Unsolved Murders

Samantha Warren Scott

Published by TruthX Publishing, 2021.

UNSOLVED MURDERS

First edition. July 9, 2021.

Copyright © 2021 Samantha Warren Scott.

ISBN: 979-8224646999

Written by Samantha Warren Scott.

UNSOLVED MURDERS

SAMANTHA WARREN SCOTT

JAN ROSEBORO

Murder happens in the strangest ways and for the strangest reasons sometimes. However, it is the murders that no one suspects, the ones that no one saw coming, that often resonate the most with family, friends, and a community. The murders that people would rather believe are accidents than consider the fact that someone they know, someone they love, could be capable of such violence stick with a community for a long time. This is one of those stories and the people of Denver, Pennsylvania will likely never forget the events that took place in July of 2008.

The Perfect Couple

Lancaster County is known for it's Amish heritage and it's peaceful lifestyle. It is also home to the small town of Denver, Pennsylvania where nothing exciting ever happens and most people like it that way. Everyone knows everyone, and everyone likes it like that. It's a tight knit community where most people who have grown up there stay and raise families of their own. There are few newcomers and there is a deep sense of trust among members of the community.

Jan and Michael Roseboro were well known members within the community. They were upstanding members within the community because the Roseboro Funeral Home had been there for decades.

Jan was a wonderful woman. She was kind and compassionate. She was a wonderful mother to four children and a loved member of the community. Michael and Jan were the perfect couple, like Barbie and Ken to anyone who got to know them.

Michael Roseboro and his family grew up in Denver. He was a typical boy who liked sports. He was an empathetic individual and cared about other people, often giving them more attention than he ever devoted to his own issues. These dispositions lead him to continue on with the family business of running a funeral home. He decided in the eleventh grade that he wanted to be part of the family business.

Ann Roseboro, Michael's mother, said that he was always great in the family business. Customers loved him and were drawn to him. His younger sister, Melissa, said that Michael was always full of energy. He always had a lot of friends and people always loved him.

The Roseboro's had known Jan's family for years. She and Michael dated for about a year before they were married. That was in 1989.

Friends of Michael and Jan could not say enough good things about them. Michael was kind and giving. He was always willing to share his wealth to those who needed it. And Jan was always willing to help out when she could. Becky Donahue, one of Jan's closest friends, said "she truly did things without the want or need for acknowledgement".

Jan settled down and started raising a family. She had four children with Michael during their 19 years of marriage. She truly lived for the kids according to friends. She was involved in all of their activities and sports. Michael also found time for sports in his love for lacrosse. He fell in love with coaching along with some other dads.

In fact, to anyone in their tight circle of friends the Jan and Michael Roseboro seemed almost perfect. Their friends indicated that they never seemed to fight. They said that they never saw Michael belittle Jan or put her down, at least not while they were out socially. They were truly the perfect couple.

However, perfection only runs so deep and there are often shadows that even friends and family are unaware of. This was the case when it came to Jan and Michael Roseboro. And even after 19 years of marriage, there are some things that time can't even sweep under the rug.

Dead in the Water

The Roseboro Funeral Home was a thriving business, and in 2008 Michael and Jan were able to expand their home. That summer their brand new swimming pool was just opened for the season and it was a cause for excitement for family and friends. However, it would also be a cause for much sadness mere weeks after it was opened.

On July 22, 2008 Michael dialed 911 to report that his wife had drowned in their swimming pool. The conversation between him and the 911 dispatcher was detached and lacked any sense of urgency on the part of Michael.

"Is she breathing?"

"No, no she's not," he said.

"Okay, do you want to try to start CPR on her?"

"I will. I will, yeah," he said.

Sargent Larry Martin was the first at the scene that evening. The police got there at 11pm. Michael said that he'd gone to bed around 9pm and his wife had stayed out at the pool. He'd woken up an hour later and noticed that the lights were still on at the pool. He'd then gone out to turn them off and noticed that Jan was in the pool not moving. He'd pulled her out and began to preform CPR as well as call 911.

Despite the efforts of CPR and the emergency response services, 45 year old Jan Roseboro was pronounced dead an hour later at hospital.

Friends and family were stunned by the events. They all had to believe that she'd fallen in the pool, had a heart attack, and drowned.

It was the only thing that made sense. They all believed that it was an accident. It was impossible for them to consider anything else.

Michael's sister Melissa came to the house to be with her brother. "Every time someone else came to the house Michael would start to cry. And then in typical Michael fashion he would pull it together. He was a funeral director". Melissa indicated that it was completely natural for him to be composed in a time of grief and crisis, it was just who he was.

Michael continued to remain composed and was even cooperative with the police. He allowed the detectives inside his home while three of his children were still asleep, unaware of what had happened in the pool outside. The oldest Roseboro child was out for the night.

The police found nothing suspicious within the home on their first walk through. It was easy to dismiss the drowning of Jan Roseboro as nothing more than an accident. It almost made sense. But the police were not going to leave it at what made the most sense. They needed to pursue the truth, no matter how dark it might be.

More than it Appears

Things are not always what them seem when it comes to the death of a person and forensic pathologist, Dr. Wayne Ross, knew that all too well. When he preformed the autopsy on Jan Roseboro he kept an open mind approaching the case. He let the body tell him a story. And after much consideration and examination it was a story that pointed towards homicide as opposed to an accidental death for Jan.

Dr. Ross found bruising to the back of Jan's neck indicative of strangulation. That was the first red flag towards homicide in this case. She was strangled using a carotid chokehold, where a person is grabbed from behind and pressure is placed on the carotid arteries restricting blood flow until the individual loses consciousness. He also found bruises all over her scalp, which indicated that she'd been bludgeoned several times. The cause of death was a mixture of strangulation, blunt force trauma to the head, and drowning.

The announcement that Jan's death was a homicide was a shock to the small town of 3000 residents, but even more of a shock to the Roseboro family who was still turned upside down from Jan's death in general.

Family and friends alike were shocked at the news that her death was a homicide. They couldn't fathom who would do this to Jan. But Michael seemed to have no reaction to the news. He didn't question his safety or the safety of his children. He didn't seem shocked or concerned that his wife's death had been ruled a homicide. And the police found this reaction to be very unusual.

His family dismissed his non-reaction as his years of working as a funeral director. They believed that Michael was simply coping with the loss of Jan in his own way. And that he was keeping his composure the way he had been trained to do over the years.

Still, the tone of the investigation changed after the announcement that it was a homicide. They were no longer looking at the Roseboro family as victims of a tragic accident but as potential perpetrators of violence. The police were now looking for a murderer; they were now looking for motive. And their attention was directed squarely at Michael Roseboro.

A Hidden Love

The day after the death of Jan Roseboro was ruled a homicide the police received a phone call from a person that originally wanted to remain anonymous. They stated that they had information to indicate that Michael was having an affair with a woman by the name of Angela Funk. It was later revealed that the caller was Angela Funk.

Angela Funk was a 38 year old, married, mother of two who worked as an insurance adjustor just down the road from the funeral home. Her relationship with Michael Roseboro started as casual meetings over morning coffee and quickly became an obsession. They didn't see each other very much, but they had a great deal of email, text, and phone conversations.

Their affair began on May 29, 2008 according to Angela and when the police confronted her about the affair after Jan's death it was just a mere seven weeks old.

Angela willingly turned over some emails and a later police investigation turned up thousands of phone calls and text messages, as well as more emails between the two. In these emails Michael claimed, not even a week into his affair with Angela that he was in love with her.

While Angela continued to cooperate with the police, Michael hired a lawyer and became less cooperative. His friends even began to question if they actually knew him anymore. He was not acting like the man they'd believed they knew their whole lives.

When the detectives questioned Michael's friends about the affair they were shocked. They had no idea he was having an affair, or that he was capable of having one. They were so used to the good-guy image that he put on that this darker side of him was extremely out of character. But the more they thought about it, the more they believed that the Michael they knew was the Michael that he wanted them to know. It was becoming quite clear that Michael Roseboro, family man and great friend, was nothing more than a façade.

Jan's niece, Lisa, and her best friend, Becky Donahue, were not surprised by the news of Michael's affairs, however. Lisa said that Michael had told her one time "I can't have another affair. I'll lose Jan if I have another affair". Becky also indicated that Jan had told her that Michael had been unfaithful in the past.

In 2003 Jan had caught Michael's affair because of a suspiciously large phone bill. And it is likely that she caught this one as well as another large phone bill was set to arrive in the mail for the month of July the day before she died.

Jan paid all of the bills in the house and a $688.12 phone bill would definitely raise red flags for Jan, considering that Michael had cheated on her in the past. It would have been over for them at that moment.

Becky was at the Roseboro home a few weeks before Jan's death when she witnessed a revealing conversation between Jan and her daughter. Jan said, "it's funny how much paperwork your dad's having at the funeral home lately". Becky believed that Jan was beginning to suspect that Michael was having another affair.

A Future Together

The day of Jan's murder, Michael and Angela had a three-hour afternoon meeting. This was their longest yet. That same day, Angela sent Michael an email that spoke of him marrying her and how it would be the happiest day of her life when he did so.

Upon reviewing the email history it was clear that talk of marriage began long before the day of Jan's murder. Angela and Michael both spoke of marriage weeks beforehand. It was clear that they were obsessed with each other, completely engrossed with each other. They discussed venues and wedding dresses mere weeks into their affair. They didn't talk about specifics when it came to their current marriages, but it was clear that they were going to leave their spouses for each other.

Roseboro's attorney dismissed the affair as nothing more than a sexual one, claiming that at least from Michael's end, the talk was mostly sexual and talked very little about a future relationship.

The emails that were exchanged on the day of Jan's murder spoke of the urgency in which Michael wanted to make Angela his wife and build a life with her. And Angela spoke about being able to see that reality come to fruition soon. It seemed to imply that she knew there would be a change in Michael's situation when it came to his marriage in the near future.

When questioned about it she indicated she was implying him leaving his spouse, never murdering her. She would never have condoned that. If she's had any indication that Jan's life was at risk she would have said something, she would have called the police.

The police knew that speaking to Angela was key to the investigation, so they continued to talk to her again, and again. Angela couldn't count the number of times she was brought in for questioning, but she was more than willing to cooperate. However, nothing she told them was as shocking as what they told her about Michael Roseboro. According to investigators, Michael had had several affairs, going back as far as ten years and Angela was simply one of many women he'd strung along. Angela called Michael from the interrogation room and confronted him about his previous affairs, which he denied to her over the telephone.

On August 1, 2008 Angela Funk revealed to Michael that she was pregnant. She was certain that he was the father because he husband had had a vasectomy. He said to her over the phone, "that under normal circumstances he'd be happy but this was not under normal circumstances". And indeed, this was far from the ideal time for such an announcement to be made.

Underneath it All

As the police looked closer at Michael Roseboro they noticed scratches on his face. They began to wonder if he had been scratched by Jan during some kind of confrontation, if perhaps this had resulted in her death. It was by no means a clear-cut case against Michael.

On further investigation of the Roseboro home there were no signs of a struggle and no traces of blood found around the pool. The lack of blood evidence could have been because of heavy rainfall that occurred on July 23, 2008, potentially erasing any evidence left around the swimming pool.

Ann and Melissa Roseboro both believed that Michael was not capable of committing such an offense. Melissa believed that it was a stranger who had come onto the property and robbed and assaulted Jan. It was easier to blame an outsider than to believe that her brother was capable of murder. Melissa based her theory on the fact that Jan was not wearing her jewelry, such as her watch or wedding ring when found, indicating that she was likely robbed of her jewelry. According to Michael's attorney there was $40 000 worth of jewelry missing from Jan's body when she was found.

So, was it a random stranger looking for some jewelry to steal or the act of a husband shopping for a new wife? As the investigation into the death of Jan Roseboro continued the case became more and more interesting.

On August 2, 2008, a day after learning he would be a father again and eleven days after his wife's death, Michael Roseboro was arrested and charged with the first-degree murder of his wife.

The Trial

Michael Roseboro spent the next eight months in Lancaster County Prison before ever talking to Angela again. In April 2009, just weeks after their baby boy was born, he called her from prison. The conversation was happy and amicable. Angela said the baby looked just like him and Michael said that it was good to hear her voice again.

The trial began on July 13, 2009 to see whether or not Michael would be convicted of the first-degree murder of Jan Roseboro. Sam Roseboro, the eldest of the children, strongly believed in his father's innocence and was confident that his time in prison would be over soon. He was not alone in this belief. Many of the Roseboro family believed strongly in Michael's innocence and hoped that the trial would bring this fact to light.

The prosecution took the standpoint during the trial that the affair was the main motivation for the murder of Jan Roseboro. They built their case around the fact that Michael was clearly obsessed with Angela and would do anything to be with her, and that anything included killing his wife of 19 years.

The defense attorney indicated that there was no evidence, no murder weapon, and no eyewitnesses. The case around Michael was sketchy at best and the motive was weak. Their case centered mostly around the fact that the prosecution had no real case, and they aimed to poke holes in the little bit of a case they had as much as possible.

The prosecution was willing to admit that building the case against Michael was difficult. It was a matter of putting the pieces together in a convincing order. They began with the 911 call. There was no urgency in Michael's voice at all. In fact, the first thing he told the 911 dispatcher was essentially his alibi. He wasn't panicked over the fact that his wife wasn't breathing. He wasn't rushing to get them to help him. He wasn't automatically performing CPR. He spouted off an alibi before anything else.

The prosecution followed this up with 1400 phone calls, over 1000 text messages, and thousands of emails compiled into a 200 page booklet that was read to the jury over five hours. This was the extent of Michael's obsession with Angela Funk, and her obsession with him. This was the motive.

Angela Funk took the stand and spent the whole day there. The prosecution questioned her about the day of Jan's murder. Angela and Michael had spent more time than ever before together that day. They'd had sex that day. Michael had called Angela and spent 17 minutes on the phone with her before Jan was murdered. And ten days after the murder, Angela finds out she is pregnant. The prosecution believed that Angela knew more, but even after a second day of testimony she didn't waver on the stand from her story.

Still, the prosecution was confident that they had established motive with Angela's time on the stand so they set to work tearing down the defenses robbery theory next.

They entered into evidence surveillance footage from a bank taken earlier on the day Jan was murdered, which showed Jan in the same clothes she was wearing when she'd drown and wearing no jewelry. The prosecution indicated that the robbery story was a fabrication created only after Michael had been subject to questioning regarding the homicide. Despite this fact, the jewelry had not been located. And the family still strongly believes that it was taken by whoever killed her.

The defense then presented forensic pathologist, Dr. Wayne Ross, who testified that Jan had been brutally beaten. She'd been hit in the head multiple times. She had a severe laceration behind her left ear, which he indicated would have bled a great deal. However, there was no blood at the scene. Dr. Ross believed that it could have been cleaned up and Michael, being a funeral director, would possess the skills to do just that.

According to Dr. Ross whoever beat Jan did so in a way to disguise the injuries. This indicated some knowledge of human anatomy and some knowledge of how post-mortem bruising worked. Michael, a funeral director, would possess this kind of knowledge.

The next most damning piece of evidence came from the scratches on Michael's face, which he claimed to have received while playing in the pool with his youngest daughter Stella. But Stella bit her nails down to the quick so there was no way she could have scratched his face. Dr. Ross was able to extract DNA evidence from underneath Jan's fingernails that belonged to Michael. This indicated that Jan had had some form of physical confrontation with Michael and had scratched Michael just before her death.

The prosecution rested after the forensic evidence was put forward, believing that they needed little else to convince the jury of Michael's guilt.

The defense put Sam Roseboro on the stand to make a compelling statement to counter the prosecution's DNA theory. Sam said that he had gone out of the house that night and while he was heading out he saw his parents by the pool and his mother was scratching his father's back. That's how the DNA would have gotten under her fingernails.

Dr. Ross argued this point indicating that if it were just light scratches the DNA would not have been lodged so deeply underneath Jan's fingernails. The presence of the DNA was the result of deep scratches. Any DNA picked up from light scratches would have simply washed off in the pool water while she was drowning.

The defense called only seven more witnesses to the stand. They left the decision for Michael to testify completely up to him and he did not take the stand. After a day and a half the defense rested. The defense did not believe that the prosecution proved anything beyond a reasonable doubt.

An hour into jury deliberation the jurors return to the Lancaster County courtroom with a request to hear the 911 call again. After a second listen to the call they retired to continue deliberation. Four hours later the jurors returned with a verdict of guilty. Michael is convicted of first-degree murder and will spend life in prison at the Lancaster County Prison.

The Aftermath

To the friends and family of Jan Roseboro the news of Michael's conviction was a victory but it did nothing to bring back Jan. And for the Roseboro family, they continue to believe that Michael is innocent of the crime of killing his wife. The Roseboro's refuse to see Michael as someone who is capable of such violence, preferring to believe that some stranger, some transient outsider, murdered her and stole her jewelry. In 2010 the Roseboro family sold the funeral home they'd owned for more than a century as they had no one who was willing to take on the family business now that Michael was in prison.

Sam Roseboro, the oldest child, chose to live with Michael's parents following the events of the trial. The remaining three Roseboro children live with Jan's sister in the same house that their mother was found dead in the swimming pool.

And across town, Angela Funk continues to live with her husband, their two kids, and the baby she had with Michael Roseboro. Her marriage is turbulent, but she continues to take it day by day.

Michael's request for an appeal was denied in 2011. Michael continues to publically state his innocence in the murder of his wife although there is a rumour that he confessed to his cellmate to being responsible. He will likely serve his complete sentence without appeal to his case.

UNSOLVED MYSTERY : THE MURDER OF HAE MIN LEE

CHAD BARTON

Whenever a horrific crime takes place it is only natural for the media and general public to draw their attention to the day that the incident occurred. In crime circles the day of such an incident is known as the "24 hour window" of discovery, but as important as this day is, often enough, so is the day before.

In Hae Min Lee's case, if we look at her diary, which was submitted as evidence during the trial, it would appear that the day before she was taken out of this world was one of the happiest days of her life. Despite her recent messy breakup with her ex-boyfriend Adnan Saed, she appeared to be in a good state of mind. And not only that, she was seeing someone new, a man named Don Cliendienst who she absolutely gushed about in her diary entries.

Even her relationship with Adnan seemed to be on the mend as the two seemed to be at least patching up their friendship, even if they were no longer intimately involved. She was in a good state of mind and seemingly a good place in her life as she expressed in her diary when contemplating her new love interest, "I love you Don, I think I have found my soul mate. I love you so much. I fell in love with you the moment I opened my eyes to see you in the break room for the first time." The day before her murder Hae seemed to be entering a happy new phase in her life and genuinely excited about the prospects of her new relationship with Don.

As much as Hae had expressed her love for Don, however, in the aftermath of her demise, as the police closed in on suspects they couldn't help but count him in as one as well. It is really just the routine process of elimination in police work to focus on the people closest to a murder victim. So, of course, the number one suspects would be a husband or boyfriend of the deceased. Fortunately for Don, the initial scrutiny sent his way quickly dissipated due to his verifiable alibi for that fateful day of January 13th, according to Don he had to work.

And after fact checking with his manager and consulting the time clock at the Lens Crafters where Don was employed, the facts appeared to back Don up 100%. The other reason that the police quickly moved away from Don as a suspect was because after examining the nature of his relationship with Hae, there just wasn't much of a motive for him to commit such a heinous crime in the first place.

From everything, they could gather both he and Hae who had just started a fresh new relationship with each other just a few weeks before, would appear to have everything to look forward to. They had not been together long enough for much bad blood or disagreement to set in, so the idea of Don suddenly strangling his exciting new love interest just seemed too unlikely. Because unless don was a complete psychopath that snapped out of nowhere for no apparent reason, the MO for Don to do such a thing just wasn't there.

But in order to find someone who would seem to have a much more logical motive in wanting to lash out at Hae Min Lee, all the police had to do was turn their attention to the spurned ex-boyfriend. Hae had left Adnan in order to spark up her relationship with Don, after all, so to investigators on the case, that alone would make Adnan Saed an immediate person of interest.

It was really here, after the elimination of Don from their suspect list that the State really began to build their case against Hae Min Lee's ex-boyfriend Adnan Saed, a suspicion that steadily mounted when Adnan's own friend Jay Wilds came to them with a startling confession of his own. And as he recounts the chilling events of that unlucky day on January 13th, 1999, Jay Wilds would demonstrate to the investigators on this case just how much of a difference one day can make.

Chapter 1: Who were Hae Min Lee and Adnan Saed?

If you hear some of their friends tell it, the story of Hae Min Lee and Adnan Saed was one that was much akin to Romeo and Juliet in which two star-crossed lovers were thwarted by their parent's disapproval of the relationship. A scene that was made painfully clear to Hae Min Lee when Adnan's own mother crashed their homecoming dance and basically publically berated and humiliated the poor girl in front of her peers, yelling at her, "Look what you're doing to our family."

It was a Shakespearian style tragedy that Hae Min Lee decided that she didn't want to be a part of anymore. But even though Hae sought to get away from the deep immigrant customs embedded in the consciousness of Adnan's family, it was something that she completely understood in the context of her own immigrant family. Hae Min Lee was born in 1980 in Korea. Her family had left Korea to pursue the American dream but the dream didn't come easy and was not free from her own internal family discord.

Her parents divorced when she was just 7 years old when her father left her mother and headed off to California to pursue his own dream, separate from the family unit he had immigrated with. Despite the breakup with her husband, Hae's mother tried her best to keep her family strong. And seeking to reinforce her family's structure she decided to move in with Hae's grandparents in Baltimore, Maryland

Here Hae would end up attending one of the toughest and most troubled High School's in Baltimore; Woodlawn High School. Despite the harshness of her surroundings, however, Hae showed that she could truly rise to the occasion. She turned out to be a bright student and was fast-tracked into Woodlawn's Magnet program.

Adnan Saed was also in that selfsame Magnet program. And it was here that the two met and carved out the same circle of friends who served as their own little social bubble within the larger social structure that they euphemistically called the "Gen Pop" (General Population) that made up the rest of Woodlawn High School.

Saed's story is fairly similar to Hae's. Although Adnan himself was born in the United States, he was the child of Pakistani immigrants who worked hard to bring a better life for their family. They sought to give their children, the opportunities that were just not available in their home country. They came to the United States for a better life, not for their son to get somehow mixed up with a murder and imprisoned for the rest of his foreseeable future.

In the aftermath of his incarceration, it was Adnan's best friend Saad Chaudry that became his number one champion. And it just so happens that his older sister is an attorney by the name of Rabia Chaudrey. It is the Chaudrey's that have become the strongest voice of opposition to Adnan Saed's imprisonment, and they have relentlessly petitioned for his release ever since his conviction in 2000.

In fact, it is Rabia Chaudrey that first brought the case to the attention of Amanda Koenig, a contributor for the radio program, "This American Life" in 2014, which then first got the wheels turning for the "Serial" Podcast. This seemingly insignificant Podcast of an untested new radio series would then become the seminal event that would lead to worldwide attention and speculation, making this one obscure case out of Baltimore, Maryland, front page news once again.

Chapter 2: Living By Schedule

Hae Min Lee was officially reported missing on January 13th, 1999. Her family filed an official missing person's report after she was a no-show to pick up her little six-year-old cousin from the Campfield Early Learning Center later that afternoon at 3:15 pm. It's every parent's worst nightmare to expect their children to be at a certain place, at a certain time, but then finding that they are unable to reach them.

And when it comes to the expected response time of their kids, all parents seem to have different thresholds of concern. While some parents may wait until midnight or even 2 in the morning before they get concerned enough to call the police, others reach that threshold of unmitigated worry and anxiety much sooner.

For Hae, all it took was for her to miss that one fateful appointment, for her family to assume the worst. Being a tight-knit immigrant family from Korea, this was just how things worked in Hae's household. When you had an obligation you fulfilled it, and when you said you were going to be somewhere at a certain time you were. And if you were not, well, then something must be horribly wrong.

Was she sick, was she hurt? With these dreadful fears in play, Hae's mother began frantically dialing everyone she knew, and as a consequence everyone her daughter knew, to see if she could find some answers. She called up all of Hae's friends, and going down the list of her contacts, she inevitably came to Adnan Saed's number. He didn't prove to be too helpful, however, and from the outset denied knowing Hae's whereabouts, but before hanging up the phone he was quick to shoot back the suggestion that she should, "Ask her new boyfriend."

Despite these subtle hints of frustration and animosity, Adnan had actually met Hae's new boyfriend on one occasion, when he showed up at Don and Hae's mutual place of work; the local Lens Crafters. During the trial, according to Don's own testimony of that day, Hae had been having car trouble, and Adnan was nothing but a perfect gentleman as Don and he both helped Hae with her struggling vehicle.

Adnan at that time, even though he knew that his ex-girlfriend was obviously seeing Don, did not display any open animosity toward him, and was actually fairly pleasant to be around. So if Adnan did have any pent up anger toward the new relationship, at this point he did not display it and was mostly keeping it to himself.

Like a perfect gentleman, truly concerned about the welfare of Hae Min Lee, Adnan appeared to be displaying the true qualities of a friend helping out his mutual friend. So how could such a cool, calm, and understanding Adnan help his ex-girlfriend in such benevolent fashion, right under the nose of her new boyfriend one day, and then strangle Hae the next? Doesn't this create a strange split in the dichotomy of his character?

Well, that seems to depend on who you ask. Because according to a former friend of Adnan named Jay Wilds, even though he appeared to be helping Hae out of the kindness of his heart when she had car trouble, it would be his own car trouble that Adnan would use as a ruse to kill her.

It was during a taped interview with Detective Greg MacGillivary that Mr. Wilds first postulated this concept. When in reference to Adnan in connection to Hae's murder, he informed the detective, "He tells me that, he's gonna do it in her car. He said to me that he was going to tell her his car's broken down and ask for a ride."

According to Jay Wilds, this was the insidious scheme that Adnan used in order to get in close enough proximity to Hae to kill her. Strangely—so soon after Adnan had selflessly helped Hae with her own car trouble—he was going to pose as a stranded motorist himself and then pine for her help. And if you were Hae Min Lee, how could you refuse? Adnan had just helped her out of the same jam just days before, who was she to now not help him when he was in need?

In this sense, if you believe Jay's story, Adnan would appear to be quite a clever and devious mastermind who posed as a good Samaritan during Hae's initial bout of distress in order to seize on what he perceived to be a future opportunity that he could use with which to gain control of, and manipulate Hae Min Lee. Very devious indeed, but the only problem is, no one saw Hae actually giving Adnan a ride.

The last time that there is any public recollection of Hae and Adnan being seen together on that tragic day of January 13th, was well within the walls of Woodlawn High School during the psychology class that the two had together with their teacher Ms. Paoletti. Hae's best friend Aisha vividly recalls the two talking together during class, but after that, Adnan seems to drop from the picture.

And every incident remembered by anyone at Woodlawn that involved Hae after this were recollections that did not include Adnan in the details. Hae's friend Debbie for instance, saw her as she was heading to her car, and insists that Adnan was not with her at the time. Debbie recalls Hae being in a hurry because her little cousin was waiting for her to be picked up from school.

The very last person to encounter Hae at Woodlawn High School was Inez Butler Hendrix, a woman who worked as a teacher and athletic trainer at the high school. Inez ran a concession stand outside of the gym and contends that Hae pulled up right in front of her, put her car in park with the engine still running, hopped out and hurriedly purchased a snack. She then hopped back in her car and left Woodlawn High School's parking lot.

During this brief intermission, Inez also insists that when she saw Hae make her exit from Woodlawn, she was alone, and Adnan was nowhere to be seen. Adnan himself initially maintained that he never asked Hae for a ride that day, he claims he wouldn't even consider it because he already knew that she was obligated to pick up her cousin and would never have had the time to do so.

But even so, a mutual friend of Adnan and Hae's named Becky claims that she did witness Hae cross paths with Adnan in the hallway, an incident in which she clearly overheard Adnan asking for a ride. But according to this account, Hae flatly refused him, saying she was too busy. Adnan would later provide a bit of additional commentary on this, claiming that, yes, he did initially ask her for a ride but he was, "detained" at school. An assertion that deflates his earlier insistence that he knew better than to interrupt Hae's busy schedule with any request for a ride.

Adnan never attempted to clarify what that detention was, continually asserting that his memory of that day, was just not that great. But after digging a little bit deeper it was discovered that he was actually in the guidance counselor's office getting a letter of recommendation for college. This letter was indeed dated for the day in question, "January 13th". And with that being the case, many have tried to point to this document as the smoking gun that Adnan couldn't have left school with Hae because he was busy picking up this important piece of recommendation.

The idea that he was getting such a praiseworthy article, which described him as having a, "warm, friendly manner, linked with his general interest in the welfare of others" also provides us yet again with that stunning dichotomy of character, making it seem beyond bizarre and incredibly unusual that someone would go pick up his high school letter of recommendation and then just a few minutes later strangle their ex-girlfriend to death, and by default make himself someone who is ridiculously un-recommendable for college or even civilized society.

Many however who still insist upon Adnan's guilt pull up the specter of "sociopath" and try to explain such strange inconsistencies with the wide brush of an uncaring deviant, who really only has his best interests at heart and who will mastermind and manipulate everyone else in the world in order to fulfill his own selfish desires. If events really play out as the prosecution said they did, Adnan would definitely be a strong case for that category of sociopathic malfeasance.

But regardless of all the endless conjecture into Adnan's personality, in light of all of these conflicting testimonies, and seeming inconsistencies, if Jay Wilds is telling the truth, and Adnan really did bum a ride from Hae, it must not have happened at Woodlawn. But then where and when could he have actually gotten in her car? Is it possible that he had met up with Hae somewhere else? Perhaps she had seen him walking down the side of the road and felt sorry for him and picked him up?

These are all questions that should have been asked when this case first went to trial because shortly after Hae Min Lee is seen by Inez Butler Hendrix leaving from Woodlawn High School to pick up her cousin, a startling gap as to the whereabouts of Hae Min Lee begins to emerge. And her usually tight schedule was tragically disrupted soon after.

Chapter 3: Jay Wilds, an Accessory After the Fact

In the aftermath of Hae Min Lee's death, former Woodlawn High School student Jay Wilds has been the only person who has ever claimed to have 100% certainty as to who was responsible for her murder. Jay told the whole sordid tale soon after being questioned by police and he pointed his finger squarely at Adnan Saed.

Jay claimed that he and Adnan had been hanging out together off and on before the incident occurred. When pressed with his relationship with Jay, Adnan has always asserted that they were never really that close. Even though they knew each other since middle school, the only reason Adnan the magnet school honor student came into contact with the much less refined, more remedial school Jay, was through the weed purchases of his friends.

Jay was a small time drug dealer and it was through this that Adnan became one of his drug buddies, with the two often driving around and getting high together. Jay also gave Adnan rides from time to time, which is exactly what he was supposedly doing on the day Hae Min Lee died. According to Jay's testimony from police who interviewed him shortly after the murder, it was on a typical outing such as this in which Adnan informed him of his intention to harm Hae Min Lee.

Jay claimed that after smoking a joint on the morning of Lee's death he and Adnan had gone to do some shopping at the mall when Adman made the chilling offhand remark, "I'm going to kill that bitch" in reference to Hae Min Lee. In their stoned state they had been talking about all kinds of crazy stuff, so Jay maintains that he "took it with context", figured Adnan was joking and didn't think too much of it.

After their excursion at the mall, Jay dropped Adnan off at Woodlawn High School. Before they parted ways Adnan had left his phone in the car and told Jay he would call him when he was ready to be picked up. Apparently without much else to do, Jay Wilds then went to his friend Jen Pusiteri's house where he played video games and diligently waited for Adnan's phone call.

As Jay passed the time with Jen, he claimed to continue his line of thought that all of Adnan's "crazy talk" about Hae was just some sort of weird, stoned humor. But when Adnan called Jay Wilds up later that afternoon he heard a lot more than the weed talking. Jay claims he heard the voice of a true blue murderer as Adnan coldly informed him, "That bitch is dead. Come and get me. I'm at Best Buy."

Jay wouldn't have to pick Adnan up from Woodlawn Highschool after all; he had somehow made his way to Best Buy. And despite the chilling words on the phone, Jay still kept his fingers crossed, hoping that this whole thing was some kind of sick joke. But when he pulled into the parking lot of Best Buy and sees Adnan by himself, standing by Haes car, with Hae nowhere in sight, he knew that something was terribly wrong.

According to Jay's testimony, he pulled up next to the car, gets out, and then is confronted by Adnan who asks him, "Are you ready for this?" Jay claims that Adnan then took him around the back of Hae's car and opens the trunk to reveal Hae Min Lee's dead body crumpled up like a pretzel in her own trunk.

Jay then asserts that Adnan then slammed the trunk shut, concealing Hae Min Lee's dead body once again, and then hopped behind the wheel of Hae's car. Adnan then instructs Jay to follow close behind him as Adnan leads Jay to the "Park and Ride" a large commuter, public parking lot, right off of Baltimore's I-70 interstate.

Mr. Wilds then asserts that they ditched Hae's car in the parking lot and the two of them went off in Adnan's car in search of more weed. It was during this search that Jay called up his friend Jenn Pusateri asking about another mutual friend of theirs named Patrick, but after not being able to locate Patrick they took off to a place called Forest Park to buy their weed and then proceeded to drive around Baltimore as they smoked pot and made more phone calls.

Some of the more controversial commentary that Jay brings to this part of his story is that Adnan receives a phone call, starts speaking in a foreign language, and then after getting off the phone comments, "It's done" and "all knowing is Allah". These would be comments that the prosecution would jump upon to try and portray Adnan as some kind of controlling Islamic fundamentalist that murdered Hae as a sort of honor killing.

In fact, honor became a major touchstone of the prosecution as Prosecutor Kevin Urick made it a point in his opening argument to state that Adnan felt as if his "honor had been besmirched."

It was after this strange back and forth, that Jay then testifies that he simply dropped Adnan back off at Woodlawn High as if nothing happened. Jay claims it was Adnan's intention to be seen at school in order to create an alibi for his whereabouts during Hae's murder. Because Adnan had track practice that day and according to Jay it was Adnan's idea to show up for track so that people would remember him being seen there.

Jay then goes on to say that Adnan left him with some final chilling comments before he exited out of the car to meet his track team, he claims that after Adnan ordered him to not tell anyone about what had happened, Adnan suddenly exclaimed, "I can't believe I killed somebody with my bare hands" and then started going on about how much more tough he was than all the other run of the mill "hoods" and "thugs" because he managed to kill an 18-year-old girl with his bare hands.

After Jay took in these strange bragging rights, he says that Adnan finally headed to track practice and proceeded to create his alibi for the day. Jay then continues in his narrative to tell the police and asserts that later that day he picked Adnan up after track practice just as planned. This immediately made the police suspicious as to why Jay was so willing to be caught up as an accessory to this crime.

When questioned as to why he would go along with Adnan through all of this, and never consider calling the police himself, Jay claims that Adnan threatened to blackmail him with what he knew about Jay's drug habits. It was supposedly in this state of duress that Jay drove Adnan back to Hae's car that had been left at the Park and Ride where her final remains still rested in her trunk. Mr. Wilds contends that Adnan then got behind the wheel of Hae's Nisson Sentra as Jay carefully followed close behind, until 45 minutes later the two arrived at Leakin Park where Jay says they dug a shallow grave and Adnan finally buried Hae's body.

Certain points in Jay's story would change periodically during the course of police interviews and the seeming inconsistency of his testimony has been a source of criticism from the beginning. But regardless of the discrepancies, Jay Wilds has continually maintained that he had nothing to do with Hae's actual murder and that he was indeed, just an accessory after the fact.

Chapter 4: Serial and the Case for Freedom

Despite many discrepancies in the State's case against Adnan Saed, it only took the jury 2 hours to find Adnan guilty of Hae Min Lee's murder, a charge that resulted in Adnan Saed being handed down a life sentence plus 30 additional years in prison. For most people in the Baltimore community and anyone outside the city who happened to be paying attention; this case was over.

Since Adnan Saed's conviction for her murder in the year 2000, for most people, this case quickly faded into the dustbins of history as another tragic story of domestic violence between two former lovers. But then on October 3rd, 2014 Sarah Koneg a producer for the public radio show called, "This American Life" and the host of a new podcast series named "Serial" managed to almost single-handedly change that sentiment of finality.

But despite her success in telling Adnan and Hae's story, for her part Ms. Koneg has always maintained that she didn't choose to cover this case, but rather, it chose her. Ms. Koneg actually used to be a reporter for the Baltimore Sun and so has some familiarity with the city its legal system. But that isn't where she first heard of Adnan's case, she first received word of the story through an e-mail sent by a certain Ms. Rabia Chaudry.

Rabia is a local immigration attorney who is well known in Baltimore's Pakistani community, she is also the big sister to Saad Chaudrey, one of Adnan's best friends. Adnan has found a staunch advocate for his cause in Rabia, and the Chaudry's have always championed Adnan's innocence, and amazingly no matter how many years had past; they never gave up on this case.

So it was that over a decade after Adnan was locked away for life, convicted of a murder hi insists he did not commit, Sarah Koneg received an e-mail from Rabia still pleading Adnan's case, and imploring Ms. Koneg to tell his story. And tell it she did, in 12 eye opening podcast episodes airing from October 2014 to December 2014.

Beginning with its debut in October 2014, Sarah Koneg's podcast on Serial shot to the number one spot on I-Tunes, breaking records with the breakneck speed in which it reached 5 million downloads and then further expanding its reach to become the most downloaded podcast in history, garnering millions of avid followers. The show even won a Peabody Award for Ms. Koneg's galvanizing efforts in bringing Adnan Sayed's story to the forefront.

It seemed that the whole nation was rapt and ready to turn the previously obscure Baltimore "case closed" murder of 1999 into the new trial of the century, just delayed by 15 or so years. Not only that, Ms. Koneg's gumshoe style detective work for the series managed to pull up some glaring inconsistencies with the state's case against Saed. Most notably from the very first episode of the podcast, when Sarah Koneg dropped the bombshell of Asia McClain, a girl that knew Adnan from Woodlawn who claims to be able to provide a possible alibi for Adnan's whereabouts on the day of Hae's murder.

Ms. McClain stated her case directly to the millions of eager serial followers that she believed that Adnan was in the library talking to her at the exact time that the State claims that he was in the car strangling Hae Min Lee. If this is true, this little bit of previously undisclosed information could change everything, and has the full potential of turning the State's entire case on its head.

Now in light of all of these new findings and supposed inconsistencies in the first trial, amazingly, Adnan Saed is finally being granted what he had been systematically denied for over a decade; a new trial. As of June 30th, 2016, beyond all the hype and hyperbole, Baltimore City Circuit Court Judge Martin P. Welch granted Adnan Saed his second chance to state his case for freedom.

THE MURDER OF CAROL TAGGART

36

OLIVIA WATSON

On Boxing Day of 2014, a young man living in Fife, Scotland walks into the local police station to inquire about his missing mother, Carol Taggart. The young man is her son, Ross. Carol Taggart has been missing for three days. Her family is desperately worried, apart from Ross, who is still going out clubbing and hitting the town using Carol's credit cards.

Then police find Carol's body, devastating her daughter Lorraine and partner Shaun.

Growing up, the Taggart family were incredibly close. The family comprised of four members, Carol, the mom, Shaun, the dad, and Ross and Lorraine, who were brother and sister.

Ross is four years older than Lorraine and had a different father, but that never mattered to them. The two were very close as children, and Ross always looked out for his sister. Both were loved and cared for by Shaun and Carol.

Lorraine, who was both Shaun and Carol's biological child, was very close with her father. She was a daddy's girl. Likewise, Ross was a momma's boy, and proud of it. Ross and Carol shared a very close relationship, but Shaun always considered Ross to be his son through and through, and to Ross, Shaun was always dad. The two shared many happy father-son memories. Shaun had taught Ross how to ride a bike when he was younger; he had been there to take the training wheels off. They were a typical family of four.

Carol and her son shared a special closeness. Although there was always enough love for Lorraine, there was no denying that Ross had always been the favorite when it came to Carol. There was always a little bit extra love for Ross.

In his mother's eyes, Ross could do no wrong. To her, he couldn't lie, he couldn't cheat. Her family described her as believing that the sun simply shone out of Ross's backside. He was the golden boy.

But in his teenage years, Ross went through some significant changes. As a child, he'd always been a loving, supportive brother and son. He was outgoing, loved to meet new people, and always seemed to be smiling. When he got older, he became very introverted.

As a young adult, Ross never said much. He wasn't a man of many words. When he was displeased, he wouldn't speak up. He would just give an unmistakable look, and his friends and family would instantly know.

For his family especially, this was frustrating. They couldn't get into his psyche, or figure out what he was thinking. They would ask him why he behaved certain ways, but they would never get clear answers from him. Most of the time, they wouldn't get answers at all. Ross would simply give them a blank stare and go to hide in his room, isolated from the family and the rest of the world.

Ross knew he didn't need to work hard to be loved by his family though. He knew he was the perfect child in his mother's eyes, he'd always known it, since the day he was born. The pair had had years together to bond before Shaun and Lorraine entered their lives. They had a mutual feeling that it had always been just the two of them.

Ross was well aware of this connection, and he used it to his advantage. He used his mother's affection against her often, emotionally manipulating her to get his way. To those around Ross and Carol, Ross's behavior showed him to be lazy, unfair, and rude. He was a user and a narcissist. But to Carol, he was none of these things. He needed her, he was her only son, and he relied on her for everything. Ross eloquently played on every emotion Carol had.

Ross was lazy in life and expected everything to land in his lap. He was brought up in a beautiful house, went on beautiful holidays, and had beautiful cars. He was used to getting everything he wanted, so he saw no point in trying to work for anything. That seemed to be his outlook on life—why try when you know it will be provided anyways.

Ross's laziness wasn't a product of his upbringing. Lorraine, Ross's sister, grew up with all the same luxuries as him, but as an adult, she worked hard to make her parents proud. She understood the privileges she had and used them to better her life and become independent. Ross was the opposite.

In the eyes of her father, Lorraine was a roaring success. She worked hard in school, achieved high grades, held down jobs, and went off to college to study dancing, which had been a lifelong passion for her. While this was happening, Ross was at home cruising through life, spending most of it alone in his room or with Carol.

Carol always saw the best in Ross. She saw Ross's laziness as a struggle. She worked hard to please him, to make him know that he was her priority. Ross knew this. He knew he could use those feelings to make his mom support him financially. More than that though, Ross understood that he could play up his role as the helpless son to draw Carol away from other people who saw him differently, especially their family.

Carol defended Ross to no end when others tried to make Carol see she was being taken advantage of, but that wasn't enough for Ross. He wanted to isolate her. He wanted to be her entire world so the money and affection would never stop.

Carol and Shaun had very different ideas of how to deal with Ross behavior as he aged. Shaun wanted to be hard on their son. He believed that Ross, who was now in his early 20's, was old enough to learn how to hold down a job and stand on his own two feet. He thought coddling Ross was holding him back from being an independent adult, but Carol wouldn't hear it. She believed that it would just take time for Ross to come out of his slump. He would grow into a responsible adult; he just wasn't ready yet.

Shaun and Carol began constantly arguing about what to do with Ross. He had begun driving a massive wedge in between his parents. For years the couple argued, unable to come to any resemblance of an agreement on how to deal with their overgrown child. While Shaun was still adamant that Ross needed to become more independent, Carol began to aggressively prioritize her son above all else, even going as far as telling Shaun that Ross came before everything, including Shaun.

After 19 years together, Shaun and Carol separated. It was becoming clear to both of them that they were no longer on the same page in life, and there was no end to their fighting in sight. Both Shaun and Lorraine blamed Ross entirely for the separation.

Shaun was heartbroken by the separation, but there didn't seem to be anything he could do. He couldn't sit back and watch the woman he loved get taken advantage of by her son, especially when he was expected to submit to Ross's wishes as well. Reluctantly, he decided to move out of the family's house.

Now, the Taggart household consisted of Carol, Ross, and Lorraine. While Lorraine was saddened by the departure of her father, Ross was elated. He loved being the man of the house. Lorraine was disturbed by the new dynamic that was developing at home and left as soon as she could. She later described the two years where it was just the three of them together as the longest two years of her life.

After her separation from Shaun, Carol began suffering from bouts of depression, so much so that she was unable to disguise her sadness from her children. In her vulnerable state, Carol was even less prepared to stand up against Ross, who began exploiting her even more.

It was around this time that Lorraine began to understand the kind of person her older brother had developed into. He wasn't a lazy boy with no ambition; he was a user. He was bleeding his mother dry. Lorraine tried to warn her mom that Ross was taking advantage of her, but par for the course, she wouldn't listen. Lorraine was terrified that Ross was going to turn against Carol one day and that Carol would be left with nothing.

Lorraine tried to get her mother help for her depression. The more depressed Carol got, the more dependent on Ross she became, and Lorraine could recognize that that was a recipe for disaster. She went to appointment after appointment with Carol and tried to get her enlisted in different facilities. But this didn't help, Carol's depression got progressively worse. She was lost.

Lorraine recalls feeling incredibly frustrated with her brother during this time. While she was doing everything she could to try and help her mom, he continued to prey on her weaknesses. And for whatever reason, Carol continued to rely on Ross more and more, ignoring Lorraine's pleas and attempts to get her help. Lorraine couldn't crack through the glass that separated herself from Ross and Carol's relationship. As hard as she tried, she was always on the outside looking in.

After years of this, Lorraine couldn't take it anymore. She relented to the fact that Ross was always going to come first in his mother's eyes, and that there was little she could do about this. All she could do was try to make her mother proud by succeeding in her own life, and it was time for Lorraine to focus on this. She couldn't keep fighting a losing battle, so she left home.

Finally, Ross had his mother all to himself. Although at this point in his life, Ross was in his mid-twenties, he had no serious relationships outside of his relationship with his mother. He had cycled through a series of girlfriends, but unsurprisingly, none of them stuck around for long.

Carol, in her depressed state, also had a hard time maintaining relationships outside of Ross. She had no interest in dating, as she still had a strong love for Shaun, and she had little motivation to make or maintain friendships.

Carol and Ross's relationship developed into a non-sexual partnership. The two began going on holidays alone together, and they began spending all their social time together, it was the kind of relationship you would expect to see between a husband and a wife—not a mother and a son.

The more time the pair spent together, the more fused their lives became. Carol was now fully dependant on her son emotionally, but

Ross was still only using his mother to make gains for his own life, and Carol was completely unable to see this for herself.

Although the family of four had been close when Lorraine and Ross were younger, there was now a clear divide. While Ross and Carol were perfectly happy in their closeness, both Lorraine and Shaun found it incredibly strange. And they were no longer alone. Many friends and family members of Carol began questioning Ross's motives. There were very few people outside of Carol that saw Ross as a good man. To most, he was a bad apple.

When Ross recognized that his mother had become fully dependent on him, he began to exert dominant control over her. He no longer felt the need to be sneaky in his manipulations; he was comfortable being outright aggressive with Carol. When she disagreed with Ross or said no to him, he would get angry and withdraw, knowing she would work hard to get back in his good books, giving him everything he had asked for initially and more.

Lorraine saw the shift in her brother's attitude towards their mom and grew increasingly concerned. He was becoming nasty. His tone when he argued with Carol was sharp, condescending, and cruel. It sent the message that he was going to get his way no matter what.

Even though Shaun had been driven out of the family home by Ross, he continued to see Carol. The pair began to grow closer again, and Shaun worked to pry Carol away from Ross just a little bit. For a while, it looked like it was working. Shaun and Carol had grown very close again, and Shaun asked to move back in, thinking they had finally found a way to mend their broken relationship. But things did not go as planned. Before Shaun could move back in, Carol told him that she'd have to ask Ross for permission.

This set Shaun off. Throughout their separation, Shaun had continued to help Carol financially support herself and their children, as her depression had been making it difficult for Carol to work consistently. Shaun helped pay the bills; Ross did not. And Shaun and Carol were adults. He saw no reason why Ross had any say in the matter. Shaun never moved back into the family home.

On August 11, 2012, Lorraine married her husband on a beautiful sunny day. It was the happiest day of her life, and one of the last happy day the whole family would ever spend together. Shaun proudly walked Lorraine down the aisle, and Carol, elated to be the mother of such a beautiful bride, was too swept up in the magic of the moment to care about Ross's dislike of her re-budding relationship with Shaun. The family was able to celebrate together openly. After this day though, Ross began to isolate his mother from the rest of the family further, something they all thought was impossible. When Lorraine had her first child a year later, Carol wasn't allowed to visit and see her first grandchild for over six months.

In October of 2014, Carol took Ross on vacation to New York City for his thirtieth birthday. Most people at the age of thirty have moved out of their parents' home, have started a career, and possibly even a family. But Ross's life couldn't have been more of the opposite, and he was pleased as punch about that. After they returned from their trip, Carol continued to indulge her son, spending over £1,500 on Christmas presents to give to him before the day even arrived. Unbeknownst to her at the time, Carol would never see Christmas that year.

Out of the blue, on December 23, 2014, Ross Taggart called the Fife police to report Carol missing. He told the operator on the other end of the line that he had gotten into an argument with his mom and she had simply walked out of the house. Because she had been suffering from bouts of depression for years now, he was worried that she had taken the argument too much to heart and had gone and done something terrible.

Investigators charged with looking into Carol's disappearance had several concerns about the nature of this phone call. While Ross sounded confident on the phone, he didn't sound worried. Additionally, he had made a point of getting information across that isn't common when people usually report family members as missing. He seemed to be trying to set up a specific scenario; it was suggestive and manipulative. Unfortunately for Ross, manipulating the police was not as easy as manipulating his mother. Investigators were wary of Ross from the moment he picked up the phone.

Lorraine had not spoken to Ross in a very long time when she got a missed call from him while out shopping with her husband. She was nervous about why he was calling, so her husband called him back on her behalf. That's when Ross told them the news—Carol was missing.

Initially, Lorraine wasn't too worried. She was hopeful that Carol had merely begun to see Ross for who he was and needed to take some space from him and therefore wasn't answering his calls. She figured she would call her mom later, and Carol would see that it was Lorraine and she would answer. By the end of the day, Lorraine had called her mother over ten times but had received no answer. That's when she began to feel an overwhelming sense of dread.

Lorraine thought of several possible scenarios of why Carol had run off and wasn't answering her calls, and they all seemed to revolve around Carol's relationship with Ross. The most likely, she thought, was that Ross had hit Carol, and Carol had gone into hiding to protect him. Despite how little she liked her brother, Lorraine still never expected the truth to be what it was.

In the days after he reported his mother missing, Ross was closely watched by the police. His movements and actions were caught on CCTV cameras and were being monitored. In the late hours of Christmas Eve, he was seen walking around the caravan park where his mother owned a holiday caravan. A few hours later he was seen withdrawing cash using his mother's card. Even later that same night, he was seen buying drinks at a nightclub, again on his mother's dime.

After Christmas Eve came and went without a word from Carol, Lorraine began to heavily doubt her brother's account of what had happened right before their mother went missing. On Christmas Day, she got a call from the police. They had found Carol's car with her purse, wallet, and phone inside. At that point, they knew something terrible had happened. They knew she was gone.

On December 26, three days after reporting his mother missing, Ross went into the local police station to check in on how the investigation was going. The visit was captured on camera and showed the true lack of emotion Ross was exhibiting during this time. This visit raised further red flags regarding Ross's involvement in Carol's disappearance. There was no recognition of sadness in Ross as he eagerly asked questions about what the police had found out so far. He wanted to know exactly what the police knew, which made them feel like he was trying to figure out something more specific—were they on to him.

Ross's actions after his mother disappeared were suspicious to everyone around him. While his sister Lorraine and father Shaun were at home crying their eyes out, calling people, and trying to wrap their brains around what was happening, Shaun was carrying out his life seemingly as normal. He continued to go out to clubs and use his mother's cards on a regular basis, even buying movie tickets to see *The Hunger Games* at the cinema. He sold Carol's expensive jewelry, justifying the act by saying he was entitled to her estate according to her will. He was not acting as if he'd just lost the person who meant everything to him just a week ago.

By January 1, 2015, Ross was the sole target of the investigation into Carol Taggart's disappearance. The rest of Carol's family had picked up on this, as he had quickly become a topic of interest when police questioned them. Initially, it was just about Ross's behavior in the days following Carol's disappearance, questions like why is he still going out clubbing? Does he have permission to use Carol's cards?

But as time passed, investigators got less subtle with their questions. Eventually, they got to the meat of their queries and asked Lorraine and Shaun the same question separately: do you think Ross would do something to Carol? Their answer was the same—absolutely.

On January 11, 2015, the Taggart family received the news they had all been dreading: Carol's body had been found.

Carol's body was found stashed beneath a caravan in the same park as Carol's. It was the same place Ross had been seen on CCTV footage stalking around on Christmas Eve. Her body told a horrifying story to police, a story of brutal violence at the hands of someone with nothing but hate in their hearts. She had been battered to death and throttled. Her neck had been broken, and she was covered in bruises. The damage was so horrific that when Lorraine was brought in to identify the body, she was only shown her mother's wrist, which had a distinctive tattoo on it, although decomposition hadn't yet made her face unrecognizable.

To both police and the rest of the Taggart family, Ross was the prime suspect. Above all else, Lorraine was angered that even in death, Ross discarded their mother. She was left outside alone, where it was cold and wet. He didn't make a mistake. He did not feel guilty. He had left the only person in the world who loved him outside in the cold alone for over two weeks, and he didn't seem the least bit sorry.

Three days after police found Carol's body, Ross was formally arrested and charged with his mother's murder. Lorraine and Shaun felt relief for the first time in weeks when they heard the news. It was unfair to them that Ross was allowed to live freely after taking the life of their loved one. They hoped that at least they could now get some answers from Ross on how he was able to commit such a terrible act.

As well as being charged with murder, Ross was also charged with perverting the course of justice after lying to police and taking measures to prevent investigators from discovering what had happened to his mother.

During his trial, which took place in Edinburgh in November 2015, the severity of Ross's attack on his mother became clear to Shaun and Lorraine for the first time. He had beaten his mother with his fists so severely that he had partially broken her neck. He then strangled her so violently that her neck snapped the rest of the way. It wasn't a crime committed from a distance. It wasn't cold and calculated. It had been done with his own bare hands, face-to-face with the woman who raised him, while she screamed out in pain and fought for her life. It was a lengthy, sustained attack, after which he wrapped her body in a sheet, put her in the trunk of her own car, and drove her out to her caravan where she stayed for several days before he went back and buried her beneath a neighboring caravan.

The case against Ross was overwhelming. Everything pointed towards him. The prosecution had been able to assemble hours of suspicious activities captured by CCTV cameras along with 188 witnesses and experts. Including Ross, the defense only presented two.

Just when the family thought they had heard the worst though, the prosecution presented a surprise witness whose purpose was to demonstrate further the lack of remorse Ross had for what he had done.

The witness was a young woman, who neither Lorraine nor Shaun had ever seen before. They soon heard that she had been contacted by Ross through the online dating app Plenty of Fish the night that he had murdered Carol. He was using the app to look for casual sex just hours after dumping his mother's body, unbeknownst to the young woman. To prove that the young woman was telling the truth, prosecutors presented the GPS log from Carol's vehicle. Both the locations of Carol's caravan and the young woman's house appeared on the log in succession.

As well as condemning Ross beyond a reasonable doubt, this information also provided insight into Ross's mindset the night he killed his mother. He was not remorseful in the least. He had felt powerful, dominant, and wanted to continue the adrenaline high he got from committing murder. He wasn't a normal human being—he was a psychopathic narcissist.

Despite the overwhelming amount of evidence against him, Ross took the stand in his own defense and denied having anything to do with the disappearance or murder of his mother. He stuck to the story he told police over the phone when he first reported her missing—she had simply stormed off into the night after an argument. His family, watching from the court, recognized the blank look on his face he always wore when he lied.

The jury in the case took less than an hour to reach a unanimous verdict of guilty on all charges. Ross received a life sentence, which meant he would spend a minimum of 18 years in jail. To Lorraine and Shaun, this was barely justice. He was set to be released from prison at a younger age than Carol had been when she died.

Carol's memory lives on in the hearts of Shaun and Lorraine, but their hearts will be forever broken. Carol had so much love in her, and it was incredibly difficult to see her taken away from them by the person that she loved the most. Ross had been her golden boy, she had given him everything she had and more, and just as those around her feared, Ross took everything from Carol. He took her money, her love, and ultimately, her life.

THE MURDER OF KARYN KUPCINET

54

OLIVIA WATSON
   Chapter 1

In the latter half of 1963, Karyn Kupcinet was living in Hollywood while pursuing her one true dream: to become a famous starlet. She was constantly on the lookout for the role that would land her her big break. From an outsider's perspective, Kupcinet was well-equipped for and well on her way to stardom. Her life had all the ingredients: she had a wealthy, well-known father, an actor boyfriend whose career was gaining steam, and dark sultry looks that many would have died for. However, behind the scenes, not all was as it seemed.

In reality, Kupcinet's life was on a dramatic downward spiral in the latter half of 1963. Her relationship with her boyfriend, Andrew Prine, was strained at best and her mental health was deteriorating since undergoing an illegal abortion in July of that year. On November 28, 1963, she was dead.

Karyn Kupcinet's life began in a much-less dramatic manner than in which it was taken though. Karyn Kupcinet was born on March 6, 1941 in Chicago. As a young child, she acquired the nickname "Cookie." That was what her parents liked to call her, so was so sweet she'd give you a toothache.

Karyn did not get her sweet side from her mother though. Esther Kupcinet was often described as not caring about anyone unless they were famous. It was no surprise when she began grooming her young daughter to become an actress. She was from the Gold Coast in

Chicago, a picturesque neighborhood that's home to Chicago's most affluent residents. Esther herself was a failed wannabe-dancer who imparted a love of the fame-filled lifestyle into her young daughter.

Her mother, Esther Kupcinet, would be the one to encourage Karyn to pursue acting as a career later in her life, but it would be her father who gave her the means to do so. Karyn's father was Irv Kupcinet, was a well-known and well-respected newspaper columnist for the *Chicago Sun-Times* who also worked as a television talk-show host and radio personality. To many in Chicago, he was known simply, but immediately, as "Kup."

Earlier in his life, Kupcinet was a Philadelphia Eagle. Kupcinet joined the NFL team after playing for the University of North Dakota. He was signed in 1935, and many thought he had a long career ahead of him playing for the team. Unfortunately, after playing only part of his first season, Kupcinet sustained a serious shoulder injury which benched him for the remainder of the season. After surgery Kupcinet was told that his shoulder would never fully recover, so Irv retired from his short run in the NFL.

After retiring from the NFL, Irv Kupcinet decided to combine his love and knowledge of sports with another passion of his that he developed in high school—reporting. Kupcinet took a job as a sports writer for the *Chicago Daily Times*. Kupcinet flourished at the job, and soon began writing about more than just sports. In 1948, Kupcinet was given his own column, *Kup's Column*, which chronicled the nightlife and celebrity scene of Chicago.

Kupcinet's success with the *Chicago Daily Times* filtered through many aspects of his career. The paper had built up his fame, and Kupcinet was now well-known in Chicago. In 1952, Kupcinet translated his fame for television when he landed his own talk show. Later, he was part of a group of talented talk show hosts who replaced Steve Allen on *The Tonight Show*.

By the time Kupcinet launched his talk show in 1952, he was almost a household name in Chicago. Thirty-four years and 15 Emmy Awards later, Kupcinet was a household name across America.

In 1957, Irv's daughter, Karyn Kupcinet, was in high school. She was 16 years old and starting to think about her future for the first time. She knew she wanted to be in the spotlight, she was a natural beauty and she admired her father's fame. Her mother suggested she pursue acting and Karyn loved the idea. She had participated in school plays since she was thirteen but had never thought of pursuing acting as a career before. Karyn soon discovered that having a father with his own television show syndicated on over 70 stations across America opened a lot of doors in Hollywood.

Chapter 2

During high school, Karyn Kupcinet decided she wanted to become a famous actress. She spent her senior year applying to arts colleges across the country and was accepted to Pine Manor College. After graduation,

Kupcinet left her hometown and family for Boston, determined to hone her acting skills at the liberal arts college.

Kupcinet's time at Pine Manor was short-lived though. In fact, the young starlet-to-be studied in Boston for only a single semester before packing back up and moving to New York City. In New York, Kupcinet began studying at the Actors Studio, a membership organization for those who are determined to succeed in the world of show business.

Through connections she made at the Actors Studio, and through connections with producers she acquired through her father, Karyn landed her first professional role in the 1961 Jerry Lewis film *The Ladies Man*. In her first role, Kupcinet played a bit part as a young lady in a Hollywood boardinghouse alongside dozens of other young starlet wannabes.

Amongst the crowd of young ladies, Kupcinet managed to stand out. The same year, she appeared in two episodes of *Hawaiian Eye*, an episode of *The Andy Griffith Show*, and an episode of *The Donna Reed Show*.

Kupcinet was getting positive reviews for her roles, and went on to guest star in many other popular television shows. In 1962 she was awarded roles in *The Red Skeleton Show*, and *G.E. True*.

As well as these guest roles, Kupcinet also landed her first starring role in 1962 on the primetime series *Mrs. G. Goes to College*, which was later retitled *The Gertrude Berg Show* for its run. The premise of *The Gertrude Berg Show* was that a middle-aged Jewish widow enrolls in a college as a freshman after her children are all grown up. While at college, she interacts with a variety of younger students and her Cambridge University exchange professor, who was played by Cedric Hardwicke.

Kupcinet played the role of Carol, a classmate of Mrs. G. who dated her good friend Joe Caldwell, who was played by Skip Ward. Kupcinet's character had little dialogue, but her dark, sultry looks stood out from the background.

In 1962, Kupcinet also completed one of her first interviews as an actress on the rise. She was interviewed by the *Los Angeles Times* to help promote *Mrs. G. Goes to College*. This interview was supposed to promote her profile as a hirable, talented actress as well, but many instead thought it provided insight into the extreme pressure the young starlet was facing.

During the interview, Kupcinet spoke highly of her cast mates and the show, but had a difficult time talking about her own involvement in the program. When the questions turned to herself, Kupcinet talked exclusively about food and her body weight.

Despite facing an inner pressure, Kupcinet won more acting roles, which she was praised for. After *Mrs. G. Goes to College* finished its short run, Kupcinet appeared in *The Wide Country,* and *Going My Way.* While her role in these shows were short, her work on *The Wide Country* garnered the attention of one person in particular—the show's star Andrew Prine.

Andrew Prine was an actor who came to Hollywood from Florida in 1957 when he first appeared in a single episode of *U.S. Steel Hour.* By 1962, Prine had hit it big. In the same year, Prine was cast in both the Academy Award-nominated film, *The Miracle Worker*, as Helen Keller's older brother, and in the lead role of the NBC series *The Wide Country.*

The Wide Country was an American Western drama about two brothers who worked in the travelling rodeo circuit. The older brother Mitch, played by Earl Holliman, warns his brother about the dangers of following in his own footsteps in the bronco riding world, but Prine's character, Andy, refuses to listen.

In December of 1962, Andrew Prine crossed Karyn Kupcinet's path when she guest starred on *The Wide Country.* On screen, their characters never interacted, but off screen, the pair couldn't keep their eyes, or their hands, off one another.

The two rising stars began dating each other, and on paper they seemed to be a match made in heaven. They were both young, attractive, and chasing stardom. In reality, however, the relationship was very strained.

Once the puppy love phase of their relationship passed, Prine was hesitant to make the relationship exclusive. They were both busy workers with packed schedules and they were young. Prine had just begun to make his mark in Hollywood, and didn't want to settle down or dedicate too much of his time to another person. Most of all, though, Prine was worried that Kupcinet would be a mar on his good reputation.

Although she was receiving good review for her work, Kupcinet was beginning to crumble under the enormous pressure she felt to follow in her father's footsteps of success. Kupcinet began abusing diet pills in 1961. Diet pills in the 1960s were not the same as they are today. Little was known about the properties of many ingredients, so the FDA often approved substances that were not safe for consumption.

One of the most popular diet pills at the time was Obetrol, which was approved by the FDA on January 19, 1960. Obetrol was marketed as a way to lose and control a person's weight. It was a popular drug at the time, and many believed that it was effective in helping them feel more energetic and lose weight quicker, which is not surprising as it was a formulation of three amphetamine mixed salts, including methamphetamine.

Along with her addiction to diet pills, Kupcinet also began abusing prescription drugs in the early 1960s. This combination proved too much for Kupcinet, who began to deteriorate. Despite coming from a wealthy family who were happy to support the young star, Kupcinet began shoplifting from popular stores and was arrested in 1963 for stealing two books, a sweater, and a pair of capris pants. Andrew Prine was mortified by Kupcinet's arrest, worried about how it would reflect on him through their connection.

By August of 1963, Karyn Kupcinet's relationship with Andrew Prine was all but over. In the previous month, Kupcinet underwent an illegal abortion in Tijuana after becoming pregnant with Prine's child. Prine had encouraged Kupcinet to undergo the procedure to protect both of their reputations and because he had no intention of marrying Kupcinet as she had hoped.

After the procedure, Prine declared their relationship over and began dating other women, but Kupcinet wasn't about to let her first love end quite yet.

Chapter 3

By the latter half of 1963, Karyn Kupcinet had lost her touch on reality. Her first love, Andrew Prine, had finally severed all ties to the young starlet due to her addiction to prescription and diet pills, but she wasn't ready to let go. Kupcinet began stalking Prine at his home, and would write about these experiences in her diary.

July 30th read, *Andy with Anna. Me watched from hedge. Awful. Nightmares.*

August 20th followed, *So humiliated by Andy's lack of interest.*

On October 29th she wrote, *Andy acting ugly. Complete indifference. Scene at his house. I'm hysterical.*

While these short messages tell a foreboding tale, the worst entries came from November.

On the 4th, after hiding in Prine's attic, she wrote *Wish I were dead*, and 24 days later on November 28, 1963, she was.

Months before her death, though, Kupcinet put a great deal of effort into making her Prine believe that her life, and his, were in great danger.

Along with stalking Prine and his new girlfriends at his house, Kupcinet began sending letters to Prine. But these were no ordinary letters. Kupcinet would put together threatening and profanity-filled hate mail composed of words cut from magazines. She sent these letters anonymously to Prine, sometimes skipping the post and dropping them off right on his doorstep.

But Prine suspected Kupcinet was behind these letters, so he confronted her. Luckily for her, Kupcinet had thought ahead and composed several similar letters to herself, claiming they had also been anonymously sent to her. She was hoping this would inspire a desire to protect in Prine, but he remained wary of his unstable ex.

Prine always remembered these startling letters. After Kupcinet's death, he had police examine the letters to see if they could determine who had sent them. The answer was no surprise to him. Investigators were able to find Kupcinet's fingerprints all over them, including on the sticky side of the scotch tape used to secure the frightening messages to the paper.

On the night of November 28, 1963, Kupcinet had dinner with her close friends Mark Goddard and his wife Marcia Rogers Goddard at their Beverly Hills House. She was an hour late for dinner, arriving at 7:30p.m. when the dinner had begun at 6:30p.m. The Goddard's later told police that Kupcinet was surprised they had waited for her to eat, and she hardly touched her food throughout the meal.

This was normal for Kupcinet though, who had struggled with body issues and the pressure to stay thin since high school. What wasn't normal, however, was the state Kupcinet was in. Marcia Goddard told authorities that that night Kupcinet acted very strangely during their last meal together. Her lips seemed numb and her voice sounded funny. She moved her head at odd angles and her pupils were incredibly small.

Mark Goddard had confronted Kupcinet about this odd behaviour during the meal, accusing her of being high. Kupcinet immediately began to cry and deny being on any substances and instead blamed her behaviour on the unsubstantiated claim that she had found an abandoned baby on her doorstep earlier that day.

An hour after she arrived, Kupcinet left the Goddard's house in a taxi cab headed home. She promised to call her friends the next day when she was feeling better. After arriving home, she was visited by two friends of hers, Edward Rubin and Robert Hathaway, who also happened to be neighbors and close friends with her ex-boyfriend.

According to Hathaway and Rubin, the three friends watched TV and had coffee with Kupcinet before she fell asleep beside them on the couch. They woke her up and helped her get to her bedroom. After this, the men said they turned the TV off, locked the doors, and left around 11:15p.m.

The men then headed over to Robert Hathaway's house where they were joined by Andrew Prine himself. The three friends chatted and watched TV until 3:00a.m.

The next day, the Goddard's waited for Karyn Kupcinet's call, but it never came. They figured she must have either forgotten or was too embarrassed about her behaviour to check in so they waited a couple of days. They hardly went half a week without hearing from the young woman, so they figured she would call soon enough.

On the third day with no call, the Goddard's began to panic, so they decided to visit Kupcinet's West Hollywood apartment to make sure she was okay. What they found shocked them both, and would forever remain in their memories.

Chapter 4

November 30, 1963. West Hollywood. It's been three days since Mark and Marcia sent Karyn Kupcinet home from their dinner party after her strange behaviour. That night, Kupcinet had promised to call the couple the next morning to check in, but she never did. Mark now feared that his good friend had died from a drug overdose.

The couple arrived at Kupcinet's West Hollywood apartment around noon. They walked through the unlocked front door and found a horrific sight—Karyn Kupcinet was lying face-down on the couch. She was completely nude.

The Goddard's immediately contacted the police, who began investigating immediately. Initially, it looked like the Goddard's suspicions had been true, that Kupcinet had overdosed on the number of drugs she had been abusing over the course of the last few years. Investigators found prescriptions and numerous bottles of Desoxyn, Miltown, Amvicel, Thyroid extract and Modaline strewn around Kupcinet's bathroom.

There was other evidence in the apartment that Kupcinet may have taken her own life; the strongest piece of evidence they found to support this was a cryptic note found in her bedroom which reflected her emotions regarding her life, her parents, her self-image, and her boyfriend.

This note was written in a haphazard fashion, a similar style to her diary entries. One of the most poignant pieces of the note read:

I'm no good. I'm not really that pretty. My figure's fat and will never be the way my mother wants it. Why must I be so alone. What's the use of living with nothing to believe it?

Clearly, Kupcinet was not in a good mental state in the months leading up to her death, and this note proved that without a doubt.

Also at the scene, investigators realized that Kupcinet had not died that day. In fact, she had been dead for several days. Her body had begun decomposing and there was evidence that flies had found Kupcinet first, laying eggs in her scalp. None of the eggs had hatched yet.

Additionally, there was some evidence of distress around Kupcinet's living room. The TV was on, but the volume was turned almost all the way down. Nearby the couch was a metal coffee pot and a brandy glass full of cigarette butts that had been overturned on the floor. A coffee cup sat on a side table across a room next to a pile of matches that had been shredded and cut up by scissors.

In Kupcinet's bedroom, investigators found that all of her dresser drawers were opened and most of the contents had been flung across the room.

Because it was clear that Kupcinet's mental health was unstable leading up to her death, police weren't sure if the mess they found in the apartment was a sign that a struggle had occurred or simply another indication of Kupcinet's mental distress. Form the scene alone, they were unable to determine whether Kupcinet had died from an attack, an accident, or an unintentional suicide.

Kupcinet's body was transferred to a nearby coroner. Sidney Korshak, a Los Angeles based lawyer that had been friends with the Kupcinet family for years, officially identified her body the next day. Shortly after Kupcinet was officially identified, an autopsy was performed on her corpse. The results of which shocked everyone in the case.

After the coroner completed the autopsy, it was determined that Karyn Kupcinet had in fact been murdered. According to the coroner, she had been dead for two days, and her cause of death was manual strangulation due to injuries on her neck that included a compression fracture to the left side of her hyoid bone with deep soft tissue hemorrhages in her neck, thyroid gland, and larynx.

After the autopsy, Kupcinet's body was returned to her hometown, Chicago, where she was laid to rest just outside of the city in Skokie, Illinois. While over 500 people attended her funeral, Andrew Prine did not.

After Karyn was laid to rest, the Kupcinet family was ready for investigators to discover who had murdered their beloved daughter so they could begin to heal. They had no idea at the time the media frenzy that would surround their daughter's murder later, or that the mystery of her death would never be officially solved.

Chapter 5

Karyn Kupcinet's death was initially highly publicized in the Los Angeles media, especially when it was discovered that another up-and-coming star was the main suspect—Andrew Prine. The LAPD believed that Prine was one of the only people who would have had a motive to kill Kupcinet. If she died, he would no longer be haunted by his ex-girlfriend who refused to let him forget her. As well, Prine strongly suspected that Kupcinet had been behind the threatening letters that tormented him.

As well, Prine had spoken to Kupcinet over the phone several times the day before she died, arguing, which was overheard by multiple sources. Prine had an airtight alibi for the night that Kupcinet was killed, but his friends, Robert Hathaway and Edward Rubin, had admitted to spending time with Kupcinet the night she was killed. The pair had told police that they left Kupcinet's apartment that night around 11:30p.m., but the only witness who could corroborate this was Andrew Prine himself.

Unfortunately, Prine, Hathaway, and Rubin had all admitted to being in Kupcinet's apartment shortly before her death, police were forced to accredit all physical evidence of them in the apartment to other times. They found no physical evidence that could directly tie either of the three men to Kupcinet at the time of her death.

The LAPD, along with Kupcinet's family, was pretty sure the three men were responsible for Karyn's death, but pretty sure doesn't stand up in a court of law. None of the men ever faced charges in the crime.

With no exciting breaks in the case, Karyn Kupcinet's murder quickly fell out of the newspapers in Los Angeles and out of the minds of its residents. It wasn't until 1967 that Kupcinet's story was thought of by many outside of her own family.

In 1967, Penn Jones Jr., a researcher with a love of conspiracy theories, self-published the book *Forgive My Grief II*, which attempted to present a set of facts as evidence that the JFK assassination hadn't happened the way the media and the government had claimed.

John F. Kennedy was assassinated the day before Kupcinet died. According to Jones, who cited an Associated Press story, an unidentified woman had called her local operator twenty minutes before the assassination of the President, warning of the impending attack. Jones believed that the unidentified woman was Karyn Kupcinet.

Jones cited as proof the fact that the call had come from California, and that Kupcinet's murder could have been connected to her spilling a deadly secret. Karyn, Jones claimed, heard about the assassination from her father, Irv Kupcinet, who allegedly had been told by Jack Ruby, Oswald's killer, whom Irv had met in the 1940s.

Irv Kupcinet continued to deny that he or his daughter had any knowledge of the President's assassination before the rest of America right up until his own death in 2003. Kupcinet wrote about his daughter in *Kup's Column.* In 1992, NBC's *Today Show* ran a segment on mysterious deaths that occurred after JFK's assassination, including Karyn's death. Irv again spoke out against the idea that Karyn had any role in the story surrounding the assassination. He insisted again that both his family and the LAPD knew exactly who had been responsible for her death—Andrew Prine, Robert Hathaway, and Edward Rubin—there just wasn't, nor would there ever be, enough evidence to prove it to a court.

When Irv Kupcinet passed away on November 10, 2003, He was laid to rest next to his daughter and wife, who passed away in 2001. Irv's death marked the end of an era to many Chicagoans, just as it put an end to the investigation into Karyn Kupcinet's death.

In her quest to be seen on every silver screen, Karyn Kupcinet lost sight of herself. Striving to be skinny, the young starlet abused her mind and body excess amounts of prescription and diet pills. When her mind went, so did her chances of finding love and happiness, no matter how hard she tried to maintain it.

Karyn Kupcinet's final appearance on television came a year after her death in 1964. Kupcinet had guest starred on an episode of *Perry Mason,* which had been in post-production at the time of her death and the following year. To many who saw her performance, it seemed the young beauty was just beginning her rise to fame, but she was already gone, taken from the world many years too early.

THE DISAPPEARANCE OF KELSIE SCHELLING

ANA BENSON

Every time a woman goes missing or is found murdered, the police usually takes a closer look at their spouses or boyfriends. It is a standard procedure, especially if there were indications that they were in a troubled relationship. The disappearance of Kelsie Schelling is one of the biggest mysteries in Colorado. This young pregnant woman was last seen in February of 2013 and the case is still open to this day.

However, Kelsie's family was quite disappointed at the lack of interest by the police to investigate her then-boyfriend Donthe Lucas, who was clearly involved in this crime. After all, Donthe did invite Kelsie to his hometown on that fateful night and he was the last person who saw her alive. When they realized that the police are stalling with the investigation, the family made a promise that Kelsie's case will not be forgotten until they discover what really happened. They kept the public informed through their Facebook page and eventually managed to reach the Colorado Bureau of Investigation.

Early life

Kelsie Jean Schelling was born on 18th February 1991 in Holyoke, Colorado. She grew up in a tightknit family and later became even closer to her mother after the divorce of her parents. Kelsie was only eleven years old when they split up but she would often talk to her father as well. However, they didn't see each other that often because he moved to a different part of town. After graduating from high school, Kelsie attended Northeastern Junior College located in Sterling, Colorado. She was fascinated with psychology and planned to major in it once she gets accepted to the university.

Kelsie was friendly and outspoken, so it comes as no surprise that she had many friends and was a life of every party. During her time at Northeastern Junior College, Kelsie met Donthe Lucas. He was a star player on the basketball team and the two of them fell in love instantly. Donthe Lucas had a very difficult childhood and he grew up in Pueblo, Colorado which is an infamous place known for higher crime rates than anywhere else in the state. He loved basketball and it was clear that he would be an outstanding athlete even in high school. Basketball players do have enormous salaries so Donthe Lucas did see it as an opportunity to help his family out further down the line.

He was hoping that a scout would attend one of his games and recruit him for one of bigger colleges or universities that had a good basketball team. But his big break never happened. Instead, he ended up in Northeastern Junior College which was alright, but Donthe wasn't quite happy with that outcome. His dissatisfaction was evident even in the relationship with Kelsie. Their romance had constant ups and downs, and the two of them would break up, and get back together which drove Kelsie mad. They did finally call it quits after several semesters, and didn't see each other for quite some time.

After finishing the two years at the junior college, Kelsie pursued her education even further, and she moved to California to attend Vanguard University in Costa Mesa. She was finally able to study psychology full time. Donthe continued to play basketball for Emporia State University in Kansas. Kelsie's family was happy she managed to end her relationship with the troubled basketball player, and they hoped that she would make a new life far away from Colorado. Kelsie was independent and she enjoyed living and studying in California. When she wasn't attending classes, Kelsie worked at a tanning salon with her best friend. However, she did drop out of the college because the school work was a bit too much for her at the time and her only option was to go back home. She moved to Denver in 2012 and started working in a store. Meanwhile, Donthe Lucas was back in his hometown Pueblo.

The two of them started talking once again during the autumn of 2012. It was obvious that they still had feelings for each other, so no one was surprised when Donthe and Kelsie decided to spend the Christmas holidays together. The couple seemed happy to everyone around them, but Kelsie did tell her friends that their relationship was still very toxic. Donthe was still treating her badly, calling her names, and starting unnecessary fights. Soon enough everything will change. A few weeks after the holidays, Kelsie found out that she was pregnant. Shocked at first, Kelsie was lost and decided not to tell anyone for a couple of weeks. But keeping a secret was hard. So she called her mother and told her the news. Kelsie's mother Laura would later say that even though her daughter felt a bit stressed, she was still excited about the pregnancy. Yes, she was young but Kelsie was determined to make it work.

Donthe Lucas didn't take the news so well. Having in mind how dissatisfied he felt about his failed basketball career, it is not wrong to assume that the news about a baby simply solidified the fact that his dreams will never come true. Kelsie noticed the change in his mood and openly told him that he doesn't have to be a part of their baby's life. But it is also worth mentioning that Kelsie confided in her best friend that Donthe was ecstatic to become a father at one point. However, his mind was constantly changing. Kelsie went to see her doctor on 4th of February 2013 and he confirmed that she was eight weeks pregnant. The baby was healthy and doing well. The doctor provided her with an ultrasound of the unborn baby, and she was full of joy. Kelsie immediately sent out the pictures to her mother, her friends, and Donthe. Unfortunately, the excitement will not last forever.

The night of the disappearance

Donthe and Kelsey exchanged several emails on February 3rd, 2013. He invited her to visit him in Pueblo. She turned him down saying that she needs to go for a checkup the next day to make sure everything is alright with the baby. After seeing her doctor on the morning of February 4th, 2013, Kelsie went straight to the store. She worked the second shift and was expected to come home sometime after 10:00 PM that night. However, she was in contact with Donthe for the entire day, texting back and forth about the pregnancy. Donthe told her that she should drive out to Pueblo after work because he had a surprise for her. Not knowing what it is, Kelsie asked for more information because Pueblo is two hours away from Denver, and she would probably be tired after work. He insisted that she would be happy with his surprise and that he cannot tell her anything over the phone.

It is safe to assume that Kelsie thought that Donthe was ready to change and start a family with her. Their relationship wasn't a standard one but it seemed like Kelsie was willing to move past all the negative things and focus on the future. So after her shift ended, Kelsie got in her Chevy Cruze LTZ and drove to Pueblo in the middle of the night. Donthe was supposed to meet her in a parking lot in front of a local Walmart. The surveillance cameras did confirm that Kelsie got there on time, but Donthe was nowhere to be seen. She waited in a parked car for almost an hour before sending another text message to Donthe, saying that she has been in the parking lot for too long and that she would come pick him up at whatever location he is at the moment. She got a reply sometime around 12:15 AM.

Donthe told her that he will be waiting for her in the street next to his grandmother's home. Kelsie is seen exiting the parking lot a couple of minutes after she got the message. She clearly did arrive at the second rendezvous spot, but once again Donthe wasn't there. Kelsie sent him another message asking where is he and Donthe replied that he will be there in a minute. This is the last known communication between these two until sometime before 04:00 AM. After going through the phone records, police did discover that Donthe called Kelsie at 03:54 AM but she didn't pick up. The significance of this mysterious phone call will be revealed later. After reviewing the cell tower pings for both phones, the investigators did discover that they were in close proximity to each other.

The search for Kelsie

Kelsie's mother Laura got really worried the next day because she wasn't able to reach her daughter over the phone. She tried calling numerous times but it went straight to the voicemail. The last message she got from her daughter was the ultrasound image of her unborn child, and Laura wasn't sure if something happened to Kelsie after work, or she was ignoring her calls. Laura contacted Kelsie's friends who told her that she went to Pueblo to meet with Donthe. With no word from her daughter, she called Donthe who picked up his phone and told Laura that he had seen Kelsie last night, but that she drove back home in the morning.

Laura was starting to panic, but she did tell Donthe that she would involve the police if she doesn't hear from her daughter soon. Laura and Kelsie were very close and they did tell each other everything, but she suspected that her daughter kept this information from her because she didn't want Laura to know that she was meeting with Donthe. After all, Laura was aware of the nature of their relationship, and his reluctance to accept the baby. Plus, Laura would probably advise Kelsie not to go to Pueblo in the middle of the night.

Laura contacted the local law enforcement and told them that her daughter was missing. Without any solid leads or evidence, they started asking around for Kelsie. Their first step was to take a closer look at Donthe because he claimed that he was the last person to saw Kelsie. She did travel from Denver just to see him. After checking Kelsie's credit card records, they did notice that the card was used hours after Kelsie's last known contact with Donthe. They reviewed the surveillance of the ATM and noticed that Donthe had the card and picked up $400 from Kelsie's account. They weren't sure if Donthe had Kelsie's agreement to use the card, but that was a felony in the state of Colorado, so he was led to the police station for questioning. He had a lot of things to clear up, starting with the timeline of Kelsie's visit to Pueblo.

Donthe's interview

After being picked up by the police, Donthe told his own version of the story. They did see each other that night and talked until early morning hours. Donthe and Kelsie got into a fight and she felt too agitated to drive back home to Denver. She was also very tired from working the second shift. Instead, Kelsie decided to sleep in her car which was parked near his grandmother's house. According to Donthe, his phone rang sometime around 07:00 AM and it was Kelsie. She wasn't feeling well and asked Donthe to drive her to a hospital. He put on his clothes, got to her car, and drove her to the Parkview Hospital.

Kelsie wasn't sure if something happened to the baby during their argument last night and she insisted to see a doctor before she heads out to Denver. Donthe sat inside her car in the parking lot for two hours when she finally emerged from the hospital. Kelsie told him that she had lost the baby. She then asked Donthe to drive her to Walmart to get something to eat and buy some snacks for the road. The two of them started fighting while they were in Walmart and Kelsie refused to drive him home. Donthe simply walked away and got to his grandmother's house on foot. He didn't see Kelsie later in the day and he assumed she went home. He didn't mention stopping at the ATM to pick up the money during his initial interview.

The investigators did notice a couple of possible leads that could collaborate Donthe's story, namely the Parkview Hospital. Each medical facility keeps detailed records of the patients they treat. After speaking to the staff and going through the data, they have confirmed that Kelsie didn't check in during the morning of February 5th. There were also numerous surveillance cameras all over the building and none of them picked up Kelsie entering or leaving the hospital. It was obvious that this part of Donthe's story was not true.

Of course, the police investigators decided to check out Walmart as well because the parking lot and stores do have surveillance cameras, and they might have picked up something that would be of use. While they couldn't find Kelsie or Donthe entering the Walmart, they did notice Kelsie's car on the parking lot. However, the timeline didn't match up with Donthe's story because Kelsie's car appeared at noon, and not in the morning. Plus, Donthe was the only passenger in the car.

Another surveillance camera which was positioned on the back side of Walmart did record Donthe getting into his mother's car – another detail he failed to mention in the initial talk with the investigators.

Without any proof that Donthe's version of the events is true, they called him up for a second interview. The investigators did have a plan this time - they wanted to find out more about the ATM, and how it fits into his timeline. He told the detectives that he took $400 in order to pay his bills and that Kelsie lent him the money since he was at the ATM while Kelsie was at the hospital. When the detectives told Donthe that there is no record of Kelsie ever being in that hospital, his reply was: "I don't even know what to say right now."

They also presented him with Walmart surveillance video that proves Donthe was the only person in the car. He was surprised with the evidence put in front of him, and before the detectives managed to get him to open up, he decided to lawyer up. He was only charged with the identity theft due to the fact that he used Kelsie's credit card, but the case was dropped. The judge had determined that Donthe did use Kelsie's credit card in the past and it was a normal behavior. However, nobody managed to figure out why Donthe had her card in the first place. After all, if Kelsie decided to ran away and start a new life, she would need the money, as well as her vehicle.

Speaking of Kelsie's car, the investigators took a closer look at the surveillance video from Walmart parking lot because they wanted to follow the vehicle. Exactly one day after Donthe left Kelsie's car there, another man approached the car and got inside by using the key. He didn't break in or steal the car. The man was dressed in black, wearing a hoodie, so identifying him was almost impossible. His body type was different than Donthe's, and the mystery man was significantly shorter. Keep in mind that Donthe was a tall basketball player, so his height would be noticeable, even in a low-quality video.

Seeing the direction in which the car went, the police collected the surveillance videos from stores and businesses which were in close proximity. They put the puzzle pieces together and found a route but they couldn't follow it all the way. One day later, the car was dropped at the parking lot of Saint Mary Corwin Hospital. The man locked the car and walked away. The investigators located the vehicle on 14th of February, 2013 and figured out the timeline. But nobody knows where the car was during 6th of February. There weren't any signs of a struggle that would indicate that Kelsie was killed in her car. Almost all of her personal items were missing, including her wallet and a backpack.

While it is unclear if the vehicle was tested for the traces of DNA, an unnamed police officer who worked for Pueblo Police Department will later say that they did find bodily fluids in the trunk of Kelsie's car, as well as two palm prints. However, no one knows what happened with this evidence and was it ever tested. It is simply another thing which the police investigators decided to ignore in this case. Unfortunately, the whole investigation will be under scrutiny soon after.

Theories

Figuring out a solid theory without too many evidence or information can be challenging. Laura, Kelsie's mother, claims that her daughter was probably murdered and that it was premeditated. The first red flag for her was Donthe's initial invitation to meet him before the doctor's appointment. When Kelsie refused, he knew that he had to act fast. Donthe lured Kelsie to Pueblo by saying that he has something to show her, but he never gave an explanation to the law enforcement about what the surprise really was.

It is clear that Kelsie was alive and well up until the point she met Donthe in the street next to his grandmother's house. This is where the trail goes cold. The activity on her phone stops until 04:00 AM. If we analyze the location of the phones, another theory is that Donthe led Kelsie to a remote location and harmed her. It was possible that Kelsie dropped her phone in the middle of a struggle. Donthe couldn't find the phone in the dark, so he had to call her number. He was very likely getting rid of the evidence.

There is a possibility that the two of them did indeed get into a fight, and that an unfortunate accident happened. However, it is more likely that Donthe planned to get rid of Kelsie, and had planned every single step he would take that night. He really insisted to see her as soon as possible. While it is not fair to put the blame on the rest of Lucas family, the fact that his mother picked him up immediately after he left Kelsie's vehicle at the Walmart's parking lot indicates that she knew what was going on. Pueblo Police Department did stop investigating Donthe, and they claimed they didn't have enough physical evidence to prove that a crime really occurred. But they did receive a couple of noteworthy tips which were ignored and never pursued.

The missed opportunities

The entire investigation of the disappearance of Kelsie Schelling was troubling from the very beginning. While the detectives did not have physical evidence of a crime, it was clear that Donthe was the last person who saw Kelsie alive. In every standard investigation, he would have been the prime suspect, and the investigators would do their best to find more proof that he was somehow connected to the crime. The cell tower pings did show that both of their phones were in a remote area next to Pueblo in the early morning hours.

But there are even bigger missed opportunities that could have provided the investigators with the proof they needed. For instance, Donthe was living in his grandmother's house at the time of Kelsie's disappearance. However, the entire family moved out soon after. The landlord started redecorating the house because he wanted to rent it again. He did hear about the missing girl from Denver but had no idea about the details of the case, or the fact that the Lucas family was involved in any way.

He decided to put the new carpets in and when he lifted the old one, the landlord noticed a strange stain on the bottom. He contacted the police enforcement because he was worried that something bad has happened in the house. However, the police ignored his request to check out the stained carpet, and no one had ever arrived at Lucas' previous residence to pick it up. The landlord ended up throwing the carpet away because he simply couldn't keep it forever in the house and wanted to move on with the renovation.

Another missed opportunity involved a couple of fishermen who were out on a lake on a night fishing expedition. It is important to mention that the lake was located near the Saint Mary Corwin Hospital. As you might recall, that was the spot where the police officers discovered Kelsie's vehicle on the 14th of February 2013. They were out on a bank when a hook got stuck to something poking out of the sand. The fishermen went to investigate and were sure that they saw a part of a human ribcage, as well as a skull.

They were terrified by that discovery and left the area right away. Both of them were reluctant to notify the police because they did have some troubles with the law in the past. But that didn't stop them from telling this story to their friends who urged them to contact the local law enforcement. A couple of months passed before they finally talked to the police, but the lake wasn't searched afterward.

The current searches

Family and friends continued to search for Kelsie even after it was clear that the police enforcement forgot about her case. They created a Facebook group that was constantly updated with new information. Pueblo Police Department did go through many changes after Kelsie went missing. The lead investigator was replaced with a new one who was willing to cooperate with the Schelling family. The Schellings did offer a large reward for any new leads that might help them locate their missing daughter. The reward was $100,000 at one point.

This eventually led to false claims and misleading messages such as the one which claimed that Kelsie was still alive, but was placed into a sex traffic ring after a hired hitman decided not to kill her.

Laura Schelling contacted the police and told them about the message. Since the investigators decided to follow every lead possible, they dug deeper and even involved the FBI. Their experts did manage to trace the message back to Russia through the IP address so it was clear that this tip was useless.

The biggest break in the case happened in the spring of 2017 when Colorado Bureau of Investigation finally got the authorization from the local law enforcement to join the search. CBI did determine that the prime suspect should be Donthe Lucas, and they got the warrant to search the area around his previous place of residence. A large number of police officers was seen around that house during April of 2017, and they dug up the parts of the backyard using heavy machinery.

The search has been successful and the officers left the scene carrying bags of evidence. However, they stated that they didn't find any traces of Kelsie's remains. Kelsie's family released the following statement after the search: "The past 2 days have been grueling and emotional, ending with the outcome we did not hope for. Kelsie is still missing. There is no way for me to convey to you all the pain that I feel right now. Sincere, heartfelt thanks goes out to the members of Pueblo PD, CBI and Parks & Rec who worked so hard on this search for Kelsie. This was a physically demanding excavation for them and we witnessed how hard they worked. Despite all the issues we have had in the past, the new leadership over Kelsie's case from PPD and active involvement from CBI is giving us hope that an effective investigation is finally taking place."

The case is still active and the police didn't arrest Donthe. But the positive changes are happening and Kelsie's family is certain that they will find the answers they are looking for now that the investigation is finally moving forward.

THE STRANGE DISAPPEARANCE
OF PATRICIA MEEHAN

86

NATHAN NIXON

Patricia Meehan Disappearance

The story of Patricia Meehan is a very strange and puzzling one. She seemingly disappeared into the night with little reason. The case has remained unsolved since 1989. With few witnesses, the full events are sketchy at best. What is well known about this case is that our culture has seemingly thought of every possible scenario to explain what happened to her. To understand and possibly solve the case, understanding the person that Patricia Meehan was is of paramount importance.

Patricia Meehan was never afraid of change. Her path of life took her all over the United States and to nearly every type of region. She was born on November 1, 1951 in Pittsburgh, Pennsylvania. She lived a typical life. She was said to have been "the perfect child" by her loving parents and by all who knew her. She had great ambition to see the world and to attack life with a smile. Socially she was on the same level as her peers. When she decided to attend college in Oklahoma City, Oklahoma, no one was really surprised. That was who Patricia was. That is exactly what she did.

She studied early childhood development and earned her degree in four years of college study. Again, she was living the American dream and successfully setting up a future to thrive. She made many friends in Oklahoma, even though it was a foreign place to a young woman from Pittsburgh. She took up a career in early childhood caregiving in Oklahoma and thrived in the profession for nearly 10 years. She was unhappy, or perhaps, unfulfilled in her work. She sporadically spoke with her family and a few friends from back home in Pennsylvania at the time. People knew Patricia to take risks. She was never afraid to change her outlook if it meant a new adventure or perhaps a new challenge lay ahead. In 1985, she made a major life change that would, effectively, lead to her ultimate disappearance.

She had informed her parents in the years prior that she wanted to become involved in animal care. She made this a reality when she moved to Bozeman, Montana in 1985. She moved alone. Patricia was not married and had left her simple, safe life behind in Oklahoma to pursue a career as a ranch hand. While this major career shift was motivated to start a happier life, it ultimately didn't always pay the bills. She worked numerous odd-jobs in the industry and could successfully make ends meet on her own. She continued this new lifestyle for four years in Bozeman, Montana.

The last person that can be fully confirmed to have seen Patricia Meehan alive was her landlord. Meehan's landlord reported to police investigators later that she seemed much more hyper than normal. This struck the landlord as extremely odd for the normally mellow, collected Patricia. Nonetheless, there were absolutely no problems between the two in any way. Patricia always paid her rent and was an "overall great tenant" to have.

The evening of April 20, 1989 is one of great speculation as to what really happened. The testimony of Peggy Bueller has always been a key component to the theories of Patricia's disappearance.

At approximately 8:05 P.M. Peggy Bueller and her father were traveling west bound on Montana State Highway 200. They were passing through the tiny town of Circle, Montana. To their surprise, they could see a set of vehicle headlights heading straight at them up ahead. A vehicle heading east was driving on the wrong side of the road. Peggy managed to swerve onto the shoulder and avoid a head-on collision with the opposing driver. The car that had been following behind Peggy was driven by an off-duty police dispatcher named Carol Heitz. Unfortunately for Carol, she was not able to swerve and avoid a collision.

Peggy Bueller had pulled over and gazed in her rear-view mirror in time to see the collision with the car driven by Carol Heitz. Thankfully, no injuries occurred in the accident. The story is very odd and somewhat eerie from this point. Just after impact, Carol Heitz emerged from her vehicle unharmed. She was shook up, but suffered no major injury. Being a police dispatcher, her first concern was for the other driver. The car that was traveling east bound was driven by Patricia Meehan. Patricia was next to emerge from her car after the impact. She stood in the middle of the road, and proceeded to slowly approach the car of Carol Heitz. According to Heitz, Patricia Meehan did not utter a single word. "She approached me calmly and silently," Heitz reported. "She seemingly stared directly through me from the moment she began to approach me."

Peggy Bueller remained in her vehicle and observed what was taking place. What she observed was "one of the strangest acts" she had ever seen. Peggy and Heitz agree that Patricia climbed over a fence just off of the road after she passed by Carol. She took only a step after getting over the fence and turned back around to stare upon the accident. She made no noise or any sort of expression. She stood there for at least two minutes. Heitz described Meehan as someone who seemed to be observing the accident scene rather than someone who had been involved in the accident. After a few short minutes, Meehan turned around and walked into a secluded Montana field into the pitch dark night. This was the last confirmed sighting of Patricia Meehan. By the time police arrived to sort out the accident, the whereabouts of Patricia were unknown. Peggy and Carol gave the exact same story in separate interviews with investigators. As eerie as the accident had unfolded, it had ended quietly and abruptly. Patricia Meehan was officially gone.

Peggy Bueller quickly drove into town when Patricia disappeared into the night. Her father stayed with Carol Heitz at the scene of the accident. Peggy reached a phone within ten minutes and alerted the authorities. When police arrived, an extensive search of the field where Patricia was seen walking away to turned up nothing. It only took police 15 minutes to identify the then mystery woman as Patricia Meehan after they ran the license plate of the vehicle. She was a registered member of the Bozeman, Montana community and had no criminal record. This was shocking to police who had assumed the woman left due to the fact that police would be arriving to the scene to investigate the accident. This posed the burning question that is still unanswered of why this woman would leave the scene of the accident if she had no criminal record.

Police made efforts to investigate the field immediately following the accident. Police discovered a tennis shoe about a mile into the field that had been accompanying a trail of footprints. The shoe matched what would have been the approximate size of the foot of Patricia Meehan. Oddly enough, the tracks seemingly disappear. Due to darkness, the investigation was suspended until the following morning of April 21. When police arrived to further check for a trail, the footprints led to nothing. The terrain had an influence in this as well as the fact that the actual shoe prints were gone, likely due to Patricia going barefoot at this point in her walk. Police had no leads.

There were two major theories that investigators had arrived at to this point. The first was the most likely. They believed that Patricia had hitchhiked from a small rural road in the area with a trucker. This could obviously not be confirmed, however the lack of a body, further clothes or footprints, as well as a lack of any whereabouts in surrounding cities points to this to be the likely case. The second theory they had suggest that she stowed away in a hay truck in the area and accomplished the same thing. This proved later to be unlikely as no hay trucks were confirmed to be in the field or in the immediate area.

The Meehan family arrived to Montana from Pittsburgh in the day following the accident. They distributed over 2,000 missing person flyers in the surrounding Montana towns and provided police with valuable information. The flyers turned up numerous calls, however none of these would lead to finding Patricia. Over 500 local volunteers searched the mountainous terrain around the accident site in an effort to possibly locate Patricia. For days, people walked the area. Some even brought dogs to perhaps catch a scent trail. These searches turned up absolutely nothing. There was no evidence of human activity in the mountains, and there were no evidence of a body or struggle in the surrounding area. Patricia had seemingly disappeared without a trace after taking a path into a secluded field. Perhaps the events in the days and weeks prior could shed some light into who Patricia was and things she had been recently going through.

The Meehan family revealed to police that Patricia had been going through some dark times in the past couple of months. Patricia was somewhat at a dead end and was feeling lost. She had asked her parents if she could return home in an effort to get back on track. Her parent's agreed, but only if she see a psychologist leading to coming home. Patricia agreed. She was diagnosed as suffering from depression. Ironically, she had an appointment with her psychologist the morning after the accident on April 21. She obviously never made this appointment.

Police also were suspicious as to why Patricia was even in this part of the state anyway. She had an appointment in Bozeman, Montana for the next morning. Bozeman was where she was living. The direction of travel she was taking at the time of the accident was in the opposite direction of Bozeman. Investigators asked the Meehan family if they had any idea where she may be going or what she was doing in this remote part of Montana. They had absolutely no idea. It was evident to police that she had no intention of returning to Bozeman to make her appointment the next morning. But could there be more to this part of the story?

The Meehan family had a roll of film developed that had been found in Patricia's car the night of the accident. The film was fully used.

There were numerous pictures of nature. Beautiful countryside and the secluded area that Patricia loved. There were also numerous pictures of animals, specifically horses, that Patricia had devoted her life to in the recent years. Patricia's family stumbled across one picture that was quite alarming. A random picture that Patricia had taken in front of a mirror. She had a very confused look on her face and seemed lost. Investigation of the picture by mental professionals led some to believe she could have been suffering from amnesia. This could obviously not be proven, but would go further in explaining the odd behavior she displayed that night. Some of the investigators pointed to this as a possible reason that she was driving away from Bozeman and was 300 miles away from home. Could she simply have forgotten how to get home? Could her mental health had gotten that bad?

Patricia had been driving on the wrong side of the road and made no effort to swerve. Police drew two possible conclusions to this fact. The first was that she was so far lost in amnesia that she simply didn't think she was doing anything wrong or perhaps forgot the basic rules of driving. The second was that she was possibly trying to harm herself or had gotten so careless that the results were not clearly thought through. These are obviously speculation and will never be proven one way or the other. The mental health of Patricia was most assuredly in a low place.

The roll of film that was developed also proved something else to investigators and the Meehan family. Socially, she was in a dark place also. Out of every picture that had been developed, not one of them featured people that weren't named Patricia Meehan. This is clearly not the norm. Patricia had mentioned that she had had a few boyfriends since arriving in Montana, but nothing serious and committal. She had previously mentioned to her parents that she had become lonely and never really made any friends in her new home. This could help to explain the depression and possible mental health issues that she had developed.

Over the last 25 years, there have been over 5,000 reported sightings of Patricia Meehan. Through all of this, only 3 of those do police feel could be Patricia or are even likely to be her. In the days following her disappearance, there were some interesting leads that were generated by the public calls on the missing person flyers.

On May 4, 1989 just two weeks after the accident, a strong lead was generated out of Luverne, Minnesota. Out of all of the possible sightings, this is considered by police and those surrounding the case to be the most likely sighting of Patricia. A police officer in Luverne claimed to have seen Patricia sitting in a Hardee's restaurant by herself. For over five hours, she was sitting in corner booth drinking water. She remained until closing time, and then proceeded to walk to a nearby 24 hour diner. Here, the officer questioned her. The woman refused adamantly to give her name. She first said that she was from Colorado, and later said she was from Israel. The major problem with all of this is that the officer could not detain her. She had done nothing wrong. However, he left without further checking to identify her. This was perhaps the best chance to obtain Patricia if this indeed was her. The officer left and where this mystery woman went next is unknown.

Another interesting sighting occurred on May 19, 1989. This is nearly one full month after the accident. A waitress at a local restaurant in Bozeman, Montana reported seeing Patricia eating there. She informed police that Patricia at in a hurry and said she had to go shopping at 9 A.M. She said she was polite, but did seem to be displaying odd behavior. Another waitress on the same shift also reported seeing her. This waitress said she was talking to herself and seemed disoriented. Patricia left the restaurant and again, no attempts were really made to investigate who she really was.

The theories that surround this case are perhaps the most interesting in the current media. If Patricia was alive today, she would be in her late 60's. This would obviously make her hard to identify in the general public. This leads to the first theory.

The first, and generally most believed theory, is that Patricia simply wanted another fresh start. She had done this in the past, albeit in a much less drastic way. She wanted a fresh start after high school, so she attended college in Oklahoma City, Oklahoma. She wanted a career change and a change of passion nearly 10 years after she started her career, so she moved to Bozeman, Montana and became a ranch hand. Many feel that she again wanted a career change and a life change at this point in her life. Turning to her parents, they gave her an ultimatum to see a psychologist before she came home. The theory suggest that she wasn't happy with her family about this. She obtained her fresh start by planning an event that would allow her to vanish into the unknown. What better place to accomplish this than a secluded highway in rural Montana where she could simply walk away.

This theory goes on further to explain that she had walked across the field and met up with someone who would drive her away. This theory doesn't sound too crazy at this juncture. The who or why is unknown, but the basis of the theory is mostly sound. Where she would have started this new life is completely unknown. But for a person who was struggling socially, not completely happy, and perhaps not enjoying the rural life as much as she had anticipated, this theory makes some sense.

The second popular theory is the more logical, medically supported theory. The collision that Patricia Meehan had was significant. While there were no injuries on the exterior, a concussion is without a doubt a possibility of this type of vehicle accident. Some believe that it was not amnesia to blame, but a concussion that would cause her to act so disoriented after the accident. The theory suggest that she exited her vehicle with a head injury and collapsed in the field shortly after beginning her walk into the night.

Montana is home to vast amounts of wildlife and has a very abstract climate. The night time temperatures in April in Montana typically are going to approach freezing. Anything under 50 degrees at altitude is going to be a severe situation for a minimally clothed, small woman with a possible head injury. The theory suggest that she was unconscious overnight and perhaps was eaten by animals, which would explain the lack of a body or any other evidence to her disappearance. It is for this reason that the theory is typically not accepted. Even with this, there would have been signs of this happening by one of the numerous volunteers or investigators in the following days.

The disappearance of Patricia Meehan has garnered national attention for the past 25 years. On November 1, 1989 the case was featured on *Unsolved Mysteries.* This would have marked the 38th birthday for Patricia.

Sightings are still reported on Patricia and a host of other in the United States. With each passing year, it is all too assuring that this case will never be solved. The lack of information on the case is puzzling. Those who choose to research the case will find that there is little information beyond the night of the accident and some significant reported sightings. All of these factors have led to a disappearance that has stumped police since that fateful night.

Patricia Meehan was an ambitious woman. She took risk in efforts to accomplish her goals and to get the most out of life. Anyone who ever knew her would say that she was a wonderful person with a positive view of the world. She loved her family dearly, and she loved her life deeply. She confidently left home to discover new opportunities on multiple occasions. It seems that life perhaps got too much for her in Montana. Maybe she just wanted to come home. Whatever the case, Patricia Meehan disappeared in April 1989, and has yet to be found. This beautiful young woman hasn't officially turned up in over 25 years. This tragic case may never be closed. A sure fact of the case is that Patricia was a sweet woman who didn't get in this situation by means of risky behavior or negative interactions. Likely, her disappearance can be attributed to a social low spot where she needed help that she didn't go through with getting. Maybe one day the truth of where her walk ultimately led will come out.

ARLIS PERRY

ROY DUNCAN

Arlis Kay Perry was a newly married nineteen-year-old when she entered Stanford Memorial Church at Stanford University in the late night hours of October 12th, 1974. She would be found the next morning, the victim of a brutal murder in what appeared to be a ritualistic killing.

Her case has remained unsolved for the past forty-two years. Various rumors and theories abound as to who her murderer was. There is conjecture that she was the victim of the Son of Sam, the Zodiac Killer, the Death Angels and the Process Church.

The police never obtained solid leads on her case and it remains as much a mystery today as it was over forty years ago.

Who killed Arlis Perry?

EARLY LIFE

Arlis was born on February 22nd, 1955 in Linton, North Dakota to Marvin Dykema and Jean Van Beek. She usually wore glasses and had her hair straight. In the lone picture of her available online, her hair is wavy and she is not wearing glasses. This is an unfamiliar look for her and no one knows where or when the picture was taken. She was small, at 5'6" and weighing 110 lbs.

Arlis would graduate from Bismarck High School in 1973 where she was a cheerleader and a member of the Fellowship of Christian Athletes. She had a high school sweetheart, Bruce Perry, and they were both born again Christians. Bruce would be accepted into Stanford University upon graduation while Arlis would stay behind in Bismarck. She remained active in her church as a Sunday school teacher in the Bismarck reformed church.

Then she came into contact with people from the Process Church.

They were six young men that were renting a home across the street from her grandmother. Their names were Father Christian, Brother

Thomas, Brother Joseph and three other men who were called "initiates."

The men tried to initiate Arlis into their religion but she soon became disenchanted with their belief system.

She realized that the were devil worshipers.

Arlis then made it a point to try and proselytize anyone who was involved in their church, leading them from Satanism into Christianity.

THE PROCESS CHURCH

The Process Cult became controversial in the early 1970s with its strong ties to the Manson family. Their belief system allowed them to worship both Christ and Satan. The church started in both Los Angeles and New York but branched out to North Dakota, as its leaders wanted the isolation of the hills and woods.

They would have meetings at the Hillside Cemetery in Bismarck and a wooded area behind Mary College. It was here that they would steal the dogs of people who lived in a nearby trailer park and sacrifice them in satanic rituals. People were complaining that they would find their dogs lying dead inside a "majick circle", their bodies badly mutilated.

MOVING TO CALIFORNIA

After graduation, Arlis would continue to participate in the Fellowship of Christian Athletes as a "huddle leader" as well as taking a job as a receptionist in a dental office. She would attend the local junior college for a year as she corresponded with Bruce Perry who was in his first year of studies at Stanford.

Bruce would return home and ask for Arlis' hand in marriage. She would accept and join him as he returned for his second year in Stanford's pre-med program.

Bruce's studies did not leave a lot of time for Arlis and she became a bit restless. She would take a job as a receptionist at a law firm to occupy her time during the day when Bruce would be away, finding work at the law firm Spaeth, Blase, Valentine, and Klein in Palo Alto.

The couple lived at the Quillen House in Escondido Village which was a campus housing unit for married couples.

Arlis got into the habit of taking nightly walks around the campus. Bruce worried for her safety and advised her not to. She stopped the practice until one night she wanted to get out of the home and mail off some letters.

DEADLY CHURCH VISIT

On October 12th, 1974 at around 11: 30 pm, Bruce and Arlis were walking on the Stanford campus. They would discover that the tire on Arlis' car had gone flat. They would have a minor argument as to who was going to take care of it. Bruce went back to the dorm and Arlis would go to the Memorial Church, telling Bruce that she wanted to pray alone.

Arlis entered and several people remembered seeing her. A security guard told her that it was almost midnight and the church was about the close up. She remained inside, however, and witnesses remembered seeing a "sandy-haired man" walk inside.

Arlis didn't return home after several hours and Bruce went out to look for her.

When he didn't find her, he called the police.

The next morning at around 05:45 am, security guard Steve Crawford would discover her body inside the church.

In Maury Terry's book, "Ultimate Evil", he described Perry's murder scene as follows:

"She was found lying on her back, with her body partially under the first pew on the left side of the alcove, a short distance from where she had been seen praying. Above her was a large carving which had been sculptured into the church wall years before. It was an engraving of the cross. The symbolism was explicit.

Arlis's head was facing forward, toward the main altar. Her legs were spread wide apart, and she was nude from the waist down. The legs of her blue jeans were placed upside down across her calves, purposely arranged in that manner. Viewed from above, the resulting pattern of Arlis's legs and the inverted blue jeans took on a diamond-like shape.

Arlis's blouse was torn open, and her arms were folded across her chest. Placed neatly between her breasts was an altar candle. Completing the desecration, another candle, thirty inches long, was jammed into her vagina. She had been beaten and choked. Death was due to her an ice pick being rammed into her skull behind her left ear, the handle protruding grotesquely from her head."

THE AFTERMATH

Security guard Crawford stated that he had locked up the church a little after midnight. He rechecked that the doors were still locked at around 02:00 a.m.

At 03:00 a.m. Perry had called the police and informed them that his wife was missing. The Santa Clara County Sheriff's went to the church and found all of the doors locked. Crawford would return to the church at 05:45 to unlock the doors and he found the west side door open.

The obvious suspect was Bruce Perry and police immediately went to brutally interrogate him.

"You knew your wife was having an affair so you killed her!"

Perry adamantly denied the questions. The police gave him a polygraph test which he passed.

Investigators would found two pieces of identifying evidence from the scene. They were able to collect a DNA sample which was found in semen near the body. The second was a bloody palm print found on one of the candles.

"It's a typical-if there is such a thing-sexual psychopathic slaying," Santa Clara County Undersheriff Tom Rosa said.

Rumors began to circulate around the campus. Some people were saying that Arlis was the victim of a satanist torture rite called the "Black Mass."

Rosa disputed the claim.

"It has no cult-like overtones," Rosa said. "It just happened to occur in a church."

There were no signs of a struggle. The detectives believed that Arlis was the victim of a "fast and sudden attack" as she entered the church around midnight.

Bruce would tell authorities that she often went there to pray when she was having problems.

SON OF SAM

Conspiracy theories would abound as the murder would go unsolved for many years. Some believe that Arlis was not murdered by a lone psychopath but by a satanic cult who stalked her from Bismarck, North Dakota.

Because of the way Arlis' body was positioned (legs spread with a candlestick in her breasts and vagina) people familiar with occult activity assumed that this was a ritualistic killing.

Fueling the speculation was some cryptic correspondence from David Berkowitz.

Berkowitz, the "Son of Sam" killer from New York City, had mentioned the Perry killing as he wrote authorities in North Dakota. He said that he had information on the killer, a man he referred to as "Manson II."

In 1979, five years after the murder, Berkowitz would send police authorities in North Dakota a book. In the margin, he had written: "Arlis Perry, hunted, stalked and slain, followed to California, Stanford Univ."

Berkowitz would claim that he was not the only person involved in the string of New York murders, hinting that he was part of a larger Satanic cult.

Detectives would later interview Berkowitz regarding Perry's murder but realized that he had "nothing of value to offer."

Those following the case, however, believe that Berkowitz should have been interrogated harder.

"Why would he make it up? He had no motive, no reason," crime writer Maury Terry asked. "He's confessed to three murders, he's not getting out."

The "Manson II" Berkowitz referred to was William Mentzer. Mentzer was suspected of being the head of the Son of Sam cult, had ties to the Manson family (although not to Charles Manson himself) and was suspected of being the Zodiac killer.

But was he responsible for killing Arlis Perry?

The answer may lie in the fact that at some point Mentzer was involved in a "hit squad" involving the Process Church. He allegedly performed assassin duties for the higher-ups who needed someone killed.

Interestingly, the serial murders of the Zodiac Killer stopped after Mentzer was in prison There were numerous parallels between the Zodiac Killer and Mentzer. Detectives believe that the Zodiac had military training. Mentzer had served in the Marines during Vietnam and killed ten people. Upon his return from the Vietnam War, the killings began in December of 1968.

The Zodiac would stab two of his victims with a bayonet style knife with rivets. Mentzer had a job where he was making rivets at a local aerospace company.

The Zodiac killer than began taunting the newspapers, sending them a diagram of a bomb while threatening to blow up a school bus. Mentzer later had a job driving a bus. He also had military training in demolition and plastic explosives. One of the survivors said that the killer spoke in a slow monotone with a drawl. Mentzer speaks the same way.

After a final letter to the press, the Zodiac mysteriously vanished in 1974.

Menzer would later be arrested for his role in the brutal murders of Roy Radin in 1983 and a prostitute/madam named June Mincher in 1984.

Radin had been shot more than twenty times in the head. Menzer would then put a stick of dynamite in Radin's mouth and blow off his face.

In the end, however, police didn't believe Menzer had probable cause to be the Zodiac killer and he would never be questioned for the death of Arlis Perry despite the rumors.

Crime writer Terry would investigate Perry's murder on his own and retrace her steps. He thinks that as many as four people were responsible for her death. He believes that the "sandy-haired" man who visited Perry at the law firm was a cult member from Bismarck, someone that she knew from the Process Church.

"She (Arlis) might have heard or seen something she shouldn't have," he said. "They may have feared she would expose them. Someone in Bismarck OK'd this, and someone had the hooks to get help on the West Coast," he said. "This was a pretty sophisticated operation."

BRUCE PERRY

Bruce Perry would complete go on to become a researcher in children's mental health and the neurosciences, becoming an internationally recognized authority in his field.

At Arlis's funeral, one of her law firm co-workers was confused when he saw Bruce. He thought her husband was a different man who had come into the workplace earlier. He witnessed her get into a "heated argument" with the man and assumed it was her husband. The co-worker described this man as "sandy-haired' which would fit the description of the man seen following Arlis into the church the night she was murdered.

Arlis would also note that there were two Bruce Perrys listed in the phone book. There is some speculation that Mentzer pretended to be Bruce Perry and had his name listed in the phone book. People from North Dakota would call and get him instead of Arlis' husband. He would then be able to finagle her whereabouts but subtly asking the family member the right questions.

This is one of the more far-fetched theories. It doesn't seem plausible that Menzer would go to the lengths of putting out a fake name and phone number just to coax Arlis' family and friends to call. Furthermore, he was a black-haired, mustachioed man who did not fit the "sandy-haired" man description.

But what is curious is that Perry's killing would be another instance of a series of unsolved murders that took place in and around the Stanford campus in the early 1970s.

A SERIAL KILLER AT WORK?

The murder of Arlis would be the fourth homicide on the Stanford campus in less than two years as well as the third incident in which the victim was a young woman out alone.

None of the murders were ever solved.

The killings started with Leslie Marie Perlov, a 21-year old Stanford history graduate who worked as a Palo Alto law librarian. She was found strangled to death on February 16th, 1973 in the foothills behind the campus. She had disappeared after leaving her workplace three days earlier.

Perlov's body would be found in a wooded gully where she had a scarf that was "wrapped tightly around her throat." There was no sign of a struggle where her body was found leading authorities to believe she walked there on her own volition.

She was not sexually assaulted but her skirt had been pulled up around her waist and her pantyhose had been stuffed into her mouth. While officers were searching for Perlov, they would find the body of Mark Rosvold, a twenty-five-year-old man out of Palo Alto. Rosvold was believed to have committed suicide the morning after Perlov was murdered. Perlov was last seen near the quarry gate of the Stanford campus, talking to a man with long blonde hair.

Seven months after the Perlov murder, physics student David S. Levine would be found stabbed to death on a walkway just east of the Meyer Undergraduate Library. The attack was estimated to have occurred between 1 and 3 a.m.

An early morning jogger would find the body of Levine. The young man had been stabbed fifteen times in the back and the side.

Like the rest of the murders, there had been no sign of struggle. The detectives believed that the young man was taken by surprise. Levine's empty wallet remained in his pants pocket and they ruled out robbery as a motive for the murder.

Levine was a straight-A student and called brilliant by his fellow students.

San Francisco Mayor Joseph Alioto believed that the murders were the work of a cult called the "Death Angels" who were suspects in the "Zebra" killings in San Francisco. Three months after the murder of Levine, a slaying took place on the UC Berkeley campus that was also rumored to be the work of the "Death Angels."

The Death Angels were a genocidal Black Muslim faction who mostly killed white people from October 1973 to April 1974. They were compromised of four black men: Manuel Moore, Larry Green, Jessie Lee Cooks, J.C.X Simon. The group committed at least 15 murders according to Wikipedia. Author Clark Howard estimates the group to be responsible for as many as two-hundred seventy deaths.

The Death Angeles would use .32 caliber pistols to shoot their victims point blank, however. They would take people by surprise but there were not any instances where they used strangulation or a knife for the initial attack as was the case for Perlov and Levin.

On March 24th, 1974, Janet Ann Taylor was strangled while hitchhiking to her La Honda home after visiting a friend on the Stanford campus. Her body was found early the next morning in a roadside ditch. Taylor was twenty-one years old and the daughter of former Stanford athletic director, Chuck Taylor.

Detectives would later concede that there were "similarities" between the Perlov and Taylor murders.

Both would be strangled although Taylor would be choked by hand instead of a scarf. Neither were sexually violated.

Both were barefoot when their bodies were found and wearing raincoats. Neither of the purses were on the person when their bodies were found.

"We really don't know who we're looking for," Sheriff's Inspector Rudy Siemssen said after the Taylor killing. "We have no motive. She apparently had no money in her purse, although you could speculate that robbery was a motive. It's a rough one."

WHO KILLED THEM?

None of the unsolved Stanford murders seem to be connected in terms of the method of killing. But, on the surface, they all were senseless and without motivation.

In the case of Arlis, there is mere speculation because of her conversations with the Bismarck Process Cult. The rumor is that someone from the cult, a leader or ordered assassin, came out to California because she tried to convert their members to Christ.

What is curious about the case is how the body was positioned. Arlis' pants were moved but placed on top of her body. The pants were positioned legs up, across her calves and her legs were spread apart. Her arms were in a crucifix position and the altar candle was shoved in her vagina.

Looking at her body from above, she was positioned in the Mason's symbol of Freemasonry. So this suggests that her murder was the work of someone involved in the Freemason cult or someone who was trying to make it look as if there was Freemason involvement.

It also appeared that Arlis may have known her killer. Her meeting with the "sandy-haired" man at work or the church may have been a scheduled meeting place. She was a devout Christian woman, used to doing the right thing, so it seems a bit odd that she wouldn't obey the security guard when he told her he was closing up the church.

The speculation is that she was meeting someone, probably the "sandy-haired" man. Who he was or how they came to meet is the question of the day. The problem is that the police failed to see the cult link in the killing, with some kind of warped religious undertones.

How much of an evangelist was Arlis and who exactly did she speak with at the Process Cult in Bismarck?

The police were never interested in pursuing that line of thought.

There were rumors in Bismarck that well-known people were part of a satanic cult that performed all kinds of grisly rituals at Pioneer Park and the caves behind the University of Mary. One witness reported that they remembered seeing people come into town in priest's outfits. Only they weren't wearing white collars. They were wearing red collars and upside-down cross necklaces.

Jon Martinson, a former psychology professor at Bismarck State College, doesn't buy the theory that Arlis was stalked from Bismarck to California.

"I remember a lot of weird religious stories going on around here in that time," Martinson said. "Like covens dancing under the full moon and rituals taking place down by the river bottoms. But in her case, I think she was at the wrong place at the wrong time."

After Terry's book "The Ultimate Evil" came out, students around the Bismarck around began trolling around the University of Mary looking for any semblance of satanic cult activity. They found none but it became an urban legend around the town. The caves behind the University of Mary were eventually filled in.

Terry still firmly believes that Berkowitz knew something that the police didn't follow-up on. "It's very important to know that it was Berkowitz himself who raised the connection to (the University of) Mary, and he did it in late 1979 – nearly eight years before The Ultimate Evil was published," Terry said. "Nothing about the Mary (University of Mary) ties to Arlis' death was made public until the book came out. But Berkowitz knew about cult activities there all along. And I also confirmed that rituals had been occurring there in the 1970s."

Ken Kahn was one of the detectives who flew into Attica State Prison in New York to interview Berkowitz. The Son of Sam killer remained vague and didn't fess up to any details. This led Kahn to believe that Berkowitz was simply messing with the crime writer and knew nothing of the murder of Perry or anyone else at Stanford.

Martinson and Terry remain adamant that Berkowitz knows something as he was documented to have been in nearby Minot Air Force base before he committed his own murders. Martinson showed Berkowitz a series of photographs from people who Terry believed was involved with Perry's murder. Berkowitz identified one of the men in the photo as someone he had met during his satanic cult meetings in Minot.

FOREVER COLD

Detectives were hoping that with advanced DNA technology and handprint databases they would get a lead on the who left behind the semen and bloody handprint.

To date, there are still no leads.

Arlis' parents would stay in contact with the Santa Clara Sheriff's Department for more than thirty years.

Eventually, however, the sheriffs would stop returning their calls.

Arlis Perry's murder remains unsolved.

THE MURDER OF ASHLEY FALLIS

SARAH THOMPSON-CARLOS

What reason would a perfectly happy and healthy 28-year-old mother of two have for taking her own life? That is the question that seems to perpetually surround the case of Ashley Fallis, who was found dead of a bullet wound in the early morning hours of New Year's day in 2012.

A beautiful young woman, Ashley was small and slight, with a bright smile and an attractive face. A photo of herself on her wedding days shows her kneeling it the grass with her children: her two daughters, Madelynn and Jolie, and her son, Blake. Her blond hair is elegantly pinned back off her face, and there's such joy on her face. It's hard to imagine that this young woman, so vibrantly fully of life, would take her own life and leave behind her three children, all under the age of 10 at the time of her death.

According to statistics gathered by the CDC, over half of American women who are killed have relations to intimate partner violence. After analyzing the murders of women in 18 different states, spanning across the years of 2003 to 2014, the CDC focused on exactly 10,018 different female deaths. Of all of those deaths, 55% of of them were related to intimate partner violence. Intimate partner violence can be described as family members, lovers, boyfriends, partners and spouses. That that definition in mind, even more chilling was the finding that in 93% of those cases, the perpetrator was a romantic partner, either current or former. It becomes even more unnerving to find out that 54% of those deaths were gun deaths.

It draws the question, with a statistical trend like this, is it possible that an otherwise happy woman, with her husband and children, would take her own life? Despite what her friends and family knew about her, was it possible that Ashley Fallis was hiding a secret depression so deep that she took a gun to herself to end it all?

Most people can't say that they married their high school sweetheart, but Ashley was one of the lucky few who could. Unfortunately, that relationship didn't last. They married soon after their high school graduation, and had two daughters: Madelynn and Jolie. Despite the children, the marriage crumbled and fell apart, and the two divorced. It was in 2007 that Ashley met Tom Fallis, who would surely change her life. Tom Fallis was a responsible man, and he seemed to have his life together.

It was only one month into their new, budding relationship that Ashley fell pregnant once again. That was how Blake was brought into the family. Their son was what brought Ashley and Tom together, despite the shortness of their new relationship. It was only two weeks after Blake was born that Ashley and Tom decided to make their family official. Tom adopted Madelynn and Jolie, and they couple married.

As beautiful a story as it seems, Ashley's family felt as if the whole thing was moving quite quickly. After all, Ashley and Tom had only known one another for a month before she fell pregnant. Perhaps their relationship had grown closer throughout her pregnancy, and then after the birth of their son. Still, it was mostly unknown to Jenna Fox, Ashley's mother, and Joel Raguindin, Ashley's adoptive father. Ashley and her mother were extremely close, much more like friends than mother and daughter. Raguindin explained how they had tried to talk Ashley out of it before the wedding.

Tom Fallis seemed like an alright guy, at first. After all, he was ready to start a family. He seemed to have his life together. But, slowly, Ashley's family began to notice that there was something wrong with him. Tom Fallis had a problem with needing to be right all the time. He was aggressive, and seemed to always be ready to argue. Jenna Fox noticed it, and she didn't like it. Ashley's family was worried by the way Tom was acting, but there seemed to be nothing to draw the couple away from one another.

After the wedding, Ashley and Tom decided to settle down together with their three children in the small town of Evans, Colorado, just an hour outside of Denver. Tom took a jobs as a corrections officers at the Weld County Sheriff's Office, stationed at a local prison. Meanwhile, Ashley began working as a respiratory therapist. Those who knew Tom Fallis thought that he took the job as a corrections officer to feed his ego. After all, he was an aggressive person, according to Jenna Fox. He was also insecure. "He wanted total control of her," Jenna Fox told 48 Hours.

Jenna Fox also felt that she was a threat to Tom. After all, she was one of the only people that he could not isolate Ashley away from. The bond before mother and daughter was, seemingly, stronger than the bond between new husband and wife. The pressure to keep a balance between her new family with Tom and her relationship with her parents was put on Ashley. That pressure only increased when Blake, only just a toddler, was diagnosed with a brain condition. The condition was chronic, and would start to require almost all of Ashley's attention. Ashley was a doting mother, and did all that she could to give her son the attention and help that he required.

The constant attention that her son required, paired with the stress of Tom's increasingly controlling behavior was starting to take it's toll. Ashley was quite anxious, and overwhelmed with the situation as a whole. Still, Fox and Raguindin had never once suspected that Ashley was particularly depressed, nor did they suspect that she was suicidal. It just didn't seem like their daughter.

Still, Ashley and Tom's marriage was starting to feel the weight of that pressure. The two were considering a divorce, but apparently their relationship was slowly getting better as the holidays approached. The couple were planning a New Year's Eve party. And beyond that, they had received happy news. As the holidays closed in, Ashley had thought that she'd become pregnant again. They suspected that their family was about to grow even more.

That happiness only lasted so long. After she had gotten that positive pregnancy test, Ashley had stopped taking any medication just in case. After all, false positives happened all the time, and she wanted to make sure that whether the pregnancy was legitimate before she continued on. However, the day of their New Year's Eve party came and Ashley began to bleed. Perhaps she had simply not been pregnant at all, or perhaps she was miscarrying. Whatever the cause of her bleeding, Ashley had been excited for the new baby. Learning that she was no longer pregnant caused her some significant sadness.

Despite learning that she wouldn't be a new mother once more, Ashley and Tom went forward with their New Year's Eve party all the same. After all, the invitations had been made, and the guests were on their way.

The part was a disaster. Jenna Fox describes the way that the tension between herself and her daughter's husband was becoming almost unbearable. Fox told 48 Hours that she "knew that Tom hated me". Despite the friction between mother-in-law and husband, the party was beginning to wind down without major incident - that is, until Tom Fallis went into a blinding rage because he had overheard Ashley's uncle offering her some marijuana. He began to swear, furious and loud. He told her that she didn't need to get high, even if she was still upset about the miscarriage. He told her, "It happened," and then told her that they were leaving, and to "Fuck everybody," and just let it go.

As Ashley's parents were leaving the party, they observed as Tom went into the bedroom, slamming the door behind him. Ashley walked them out, and they said their goodbyes at 12:04 am, after the New Year's ball had already dropped. Fox didn't observe anything out of the ordinary about her daughter. She didn't seem upset by Tom's behavior, after all. It wasn't out of place for Tom to act like this, and become enraged and swear. As Fox and Raguindin hugged their daughter and said their goodbyes on the front porch, they had no idea that this would be the last time that they saw their daughter alive.

Ashley isn't here any longer to tell us the rest of her story. What we know of that night is what Tom Fallis claims happened, and the autopsy reports, and the police records. As they guests filtered out of the house, they were among the last to see Ashley Fallis alive. When the last guest left and the door closed, no one but Ashley and Tom Fallis really know what happened that night that lead to the death of Ashley early in the hours of New Year's Day.

According to Tom Fallis, Ashley came into the bedroom in a defiant mood, and he said that she told him that if she wanted to get high, then she would get high. Tom told police that he told her to do whatever she wanted. Tom told the police that he had been in their closet, getting changed, when he heard the sound of her loading a gun across the room. Supposedly, it was the .9mm Taurus that Ashley kept under her mattress. As Tom walked out of the closet, he asked her what she was doing - and then, he heard the sound of a gunshot. Tom claims that he ran across the room to where Ashley was and held her head where the gunshot wound was, then grabbed the phone and dialed 911.

A recording of Tom Fallis' panicked 911 call plays Tom's voice, panicked and screaming: "My wife just shot herself in the head! Please help me! Please help me!" While the 911 operator tries to get his exact location and calm him down, Tom's voice comes through the call, tinny and screaming: "Ashley, no! Ashley, no!"

Finally, as the 911 operator tries to get more information, Tom can be heard shouting at his dying wife: "You are not leaving me! You are not leaving me! Stay right here!"

All in all, Ashley's family had only been gone for ten minutes. Ten minutes previous, Ashley had been on the porch, saying goodbye to all of her loved ones after celebrating the incoming of the new year. Her parents weren't even home, yet. They were still on the road when they saw the squad cars that were dispatched due to the call made by Tom.

At the hospital, Jenna Fox told 48 Hours that she knew, from the moment that she had seen her daughter lying in the hospital bed, that Tom Fallis had been involved. Perhaps it was a mother's intuition. Whatever the reason, Fox had no doubt that her daughter wouldn't have committed suicide. Even with the grief of her miscarriage hanging heavy over her that New Year's Eve, she was surrounded by her family and loved ones. Fox didn't believe for one second that suicide was an option for her daughter.

Ashley Fallis hadn't died immediately from that gunshot wound. She arrived at the hospital with severe trauma to the brain. But she wouldn't recover. The last time that her parents saw her alive and sentient was on the porch, ten minutes before she took a gunshot wound to the head.

But what happened? Tom's versions of events are clear. Ashley came into the bedroom, angry, and took a gun to her own head. Despite the fact that statistics put female suicides by firearm at only 31.2% (compared to male suicide by firearm at 56.4%), is it possible that Ashley had chosen such method? Women who commit suicide are often going to chose a less painful method, and one that would not leave behind such a mess. Pills and cutting of the wrists are much more popular methods when it comes to women who take their own life. But perhaps it was Ashley's grief that had driven her to take her own life with the gun she kept under her mattress.

Was it?

Despite the fact that Tom Fallis called in a suicide to 911, the police thought that it was important to question him about what happened. The police brought Tom Fallis into the station early on the morning of New Year's day, leaving his parents to watch his and Ashley's three small children. While Tom's frantic 911 call had seemed genuine, the police weren't all too sure. Neighbors had reported that they could hearing yelling and arguing coming from the couples house. Being questioned by Detective Rita Wolf, Tom was immediately put under scrutiny. The wound on Ashley's head was near the back. When told that her wound wasn't consistent with a suicide shot, Tom simply replied, "Bullshit! I didn't shoot my wife."

When investigators searched Tom's body, they found scratches on his chest, which he had said were from himself itching at his newly shaved chest. But that's not all investigators found. When they went into the Fallis' residence to take stock of the scene of the suicide, they discovered something strange. Tom's version of events had Ashley coming into the bedroom in an agitated state, then simply going across the room to retrieve her gun from under her mattress and shoot herself in the head. The state of the house, however, was inconsistent with that story.

Investigators found that pictures had been strewn from their place on the wall. It looked as if there had been a struggle. Not only that, but divorce papers had been found placed in a drawer. Tom Fallis had insisted that things had been going alright with him and Ashley, and that while they had been struggling before, things were moving in the right direction. The mere presence of divorce papers seemed to speak volumes, going against what Tom Fallis claimed was going on in his supposedly happy family.

At the hospital, Ashley Fallis had bruises on her legs. All of the evidence that investigators were digging up seemed to show that something else had gone down after all the guests had left the party - and that it wasn't suicide. Still, even after Tom Fallis was questioned for hours, he was released later that morning without charges being pressed against him.

Raguindin told 48 Hours that he and Fox were "shocked that they let him go." Even more shocking was what happened after that. Detective Wolf had told Tom Fallis that she didn't believe that Ashley could have inflicted that gunshot wound on herself. The position of the wound at the back of her head wasn't consistent with a suicide. Still, on January 5th, the coroner made an official ruling, and Ashley's death was listed as a suicide. Officially, the case was closed.

That seemed to be that. Ashley Fallis, wife, mother of three and devoted caretaker of her special needs son, was said to have taken her own life in the early morning hours of January 1st, ten minutes after waving goodbye to her family on the front porch after their New Year's Eve party.

The story for Tom Fallis, however, would go on. He packed up his children and moved them to Indiana, where he would attend graduate school. Despite the stress and strain of the relationship between Tom and Ashley's parents, they were determined to keep in contact with him for the sake of continuing a relationship with their grandchildren. After all, they were the only pieces of their daughter that they had left.

Life went on. For two years, Ashley's parents mourned their daughter's untimely death, and maintained a relationship with a man that they hated for the sake of their grandchildren. It seemed like no one else believed that Ashley wouldn't have taken her own life, and no one else believed that Tom Fallis was at fault. Until, one day, two years after Ashley's death, a man named Justin Joseph caught wind of the case. Joseph was a television news reporter with a source in law enforcement. Turns out, Ashley's parents weren't the only ones who were perturbed by the case.

Two years had passed, but Joseph took on investigating Ashley's story, anyway. Nothing seemed to sit right, and it was finally time to bring Ashley the justice that she deserved. Months were put into interviewing neighbors and friends who had already been cleared by the police, all of their statements taken and their concerns brushed off. In April of 2014, Joseph interviewed one of the Fallis' next door neighbors, Nick Glover, and found just what he needed to bust the case of Ashley's death wide open again.

Glover's versions of events differed from Tom Fallis'. According to Glover, he had heard Tom come out of the house, so he knelt down beneath the window sill to stay out of sight while he listened. Tom's parents were outside, and Glover could hear Tom saying, "Oh my god, I can't believe I did it." When his parents pressed him for more information, Glover heard Tom say: "I shot her." Of course, this wasn't the first time that Glover had told someone what had happened. In fact, the day that he was questioned by Evans Police, Glover told exactly the same thing to a Detective Michael Yates.

Glover's mother, Kathy Glover, had gotten a phone call that night from another neighbor by the name of Chelsey Arrigo. She told them to call the police, because she was sure that Tom Fallis had just shot his wife. Arrigo had heard Ashley yelling for Tom to get off of her, and the pop of the gun.

Everyone seemed to know what happened that night, and nothing was done. In fact, Detective Yates hadn't even written the report correctly. In his report of the incident that night, he quoted Arrigo as saying Ashley shot herself, not that Tom Fallis had shot her. Yates had also claimed that Glover had never told him about overhearing Tom admit to the murder of his wife. With contradicting statements, no one knew why a follow-up hadn't been given. Arrigo hadn't even been interviewed, despite knowing that Kathy had been in contact with her the night of Ashley's death. The case had been handled poorly from open to close, and no one seemed to know why.

Joseph found another person who had heard Tom Fallis admit the the murder of his wife: a sheriff's deputy who happened to be at the scene. It wasn't until two years later that he came forward to tell the investigators what he head heard. It's unclear as to why the case of Ashley Fallis wasn't treated as a homicide, or why no one seemed to take Glover seriously when he had told them what he heard, or why the sheriff's deputy said nothing to anyone until two years after the fact.

Was it a cover-up by the police? Or was it simply serious human error that caused the police not to go back and re-interview the people who had said they heard Tom Fallis admitting to murder? It seems hard to believe that the police would simply brush away Detective Wolf pointing out the position of the gunshot wound on Ashley's head, and two witnesses who had heard Tom Fallis saying clearly, "I shot her." One would want to hope that it was a serious error, and not the police deliberately looking the other way. There's no explanation for why Ashley Fallis' death was ruled a suicide, despite the evidence of a struggle in their house, and the witnesses that described Tom Fallis has raging and angry that night.

Whatever the reason that Ashley's case was closed, it was Justin Joseph that got it re-opened. His investigating opened up some serious questions about that night, and why the police had moved forward to rule her death a suicide. The case was reopened by a Evans, Colorado neighbor, Fort Collins, along with their much larger police force.

Tom Fallis had more information for the police, too. Two years after Ashley's death, Tom Fallis came forward during the new investigation with a suicide note that Ashley had supposedly written. There were several notes, one which read: "Dear Tom [...] I'm sorry for your pain. [...] I am a failure at everything." Of course, the timing of the suicide notes were suspicious. If Ashley had committed suicide, wouldn't the notes have shown up that first night?

Finally, it seemed like justice for Ashley Fallis was going to happen. In November of 2014, a grand jury made the decision to indict Tom Fallis for the murder of his wife. He was arrested in Indiana, and his children were put under the care of his parents. Tom Fallis had gotten away with putting his wife's supposed suicide in the past for almost three years. It wasn't until March of 2016 that Tom was finally put on trial.

The defense used Ashley's history of mental illness, anxiety, and the pain of her miscarriage to build a case against a dead woman. They claimed that it was Ashley who had shot herself in the middle of a crisis that early morning on New Year's Day. They pointed out that Ashley had been drinking at the party, and that there was even a history of suicide in her family: her uncle's mother and brother both died from suicide by gunshot. Was this just another suicide in a long line of tragedies? The defense seemed to think so.

Still, when Ashley's therapist took the stand, he made it clear that he did not consider Ashley a danger to herself or others. Still, Ashley was on medications from other doctors that she didn't tell her therapist. Defense used that against her, and in favor of Tom - saying it was entirely possible that Ashley Fallis could have written those suicide notes without telling her therapist.

When Ashley's parents were finally able to take the stand, they insisted that Ashley was fine throughout the night. Despite her miscarriage earlier in the day, Ashley was among family and friends. Her demeanor only changed when Tom became volatile. Jenna Fox described, once more, how Tom Fallis swore at them all and wished for them all to die before going into the bedroom and slamming the door.

Nick Glover also took the stand, repeating what he heard outside of his window that night. Tom Fallis' parents, however, denied that Tom had told them that he shot his wife. Kathy Glover also reiterated the phone call she got at one in the morning from Chelsey Arrigo. Unfortunately, when Arrigo took the stand, she couldn't remember making such a statement to Kathy Glover. All she remembered was hearing some arguing. Apparently, Arrigo was intoxicated because of her own New Year's celebration. Weld County Sheriff's Deputy, Chris Graves, was able to testify that he also heard with Nick Glover had heard that night, which was Tom Fallis admitting to shooting his wife. Still, he was questioned pretty hard after admitting that he should have come forward about it sooner than two years after the fact.

Forensic evidence didn't fair well in Ashley's favor, either. It was determined that the gunshot would very well could have been self inflicted. And yet, the prosecution called forward a forensic expert of their own, Jon Priest, who explained the exact opposite: no, Ashley's gunshot wound could not have been self inflicted.

There was so much testimony and evidence that the jury had to go through. The conflicting theories from the defense and the prosecution told two entirely different stories about what happened that night to Ashley Fallis. When the Jury retreated to deliberate the case and make their verdict, it didn't take them very long. In fact, the jury was only out for about three and a half hours. When they finally came back, Ashley's family could only wait with baited breath as the jury read out their decision.

Not guilty.

Tom Fallis was acquitted on the murder of his beloved wife, mother of his children. Ashley's family still holds their opinion that their daughter would never take her own life, and Justin Joseph maintains that the entire case of Ashley's death was handled poorly from start to finish. There was reasonable doubt that Ashley had killed herself that night, and there was no follow up done. Still, even after all the evidence was presented, the jury could not find Tom Fallis guilty. Whatever happened to Ashley Fallis that night will only ever be known by two people: Ashley and Tom.

THE LIFE AND MURDER OF HOLLY BOBO

125

ASHLEY CORDERO

It seemed that Holly Lynn Bobo (born October 12, 1990) had it all, and could do just about anything she set her mind to. The Southern belle had a great circle of friends, a loving family, a devoted boyfriend and a bright future ahead. She lived with her family in the tiny town of Darden, Tennessee on a pretty property on the edge of some woods. Hailing from the Bible Belt, Holly was heavily involved in her church community. She had the face of an angel, but wasn't content to just coast by on her good looks. Always one to help other people, Holly was a dedicated nursing student at the University of Tennessee at Martin. She was also a talented singer. It was in her blood – she is a first cousin to reality television star and country singer / songwriter Whitney Duncan. Holly was what is referred to as a big fish in a small pond. In short, this was a young woman who was going places.

However, on April 13, 2011, the 20-year-old's seemingly charmed life was about to turn into a nightmare. Holly had set her alarm for 4.30 a.m. in order to do some last minute cramming for a nursing exam. She awoke, ate breakfast, studied and dressed for school. At 7.30 a.m. Holly took a short phone call from her boyfriend, Drew Scott. He was nearby doing some early morning turkey hunting on Holly's grandmother's property, and called to wish her good luck on her exam. By this stage Holly's parents were both already at work and her brother Clint was still sleeping in his bedroom.

Ten minutes later, the Bobos' neighbor heard the sound of a young woman screaming. It seemed to come from the Bobo residence. Concerned, the neighbor informed her mother. The mother telephoned Karen Bobo (Holly's mother) straight away at her place of business and reported what her daughter had heard. While this was going on, Clint Bobo was roused from his slumber by the din of the Bobo family dogs barking at something. Peering out of a crack in his blinds he saw a man with Holly outside. He would later tell the media 'It appeared to be Holly kneeling down and Drew. They looked like they were kneeled down, facing each other in the garage, and they were talking back and forth. Holly sounded very upset and heated. He was doing much of the talking, and she would answer back and things like that. I couldn't make out hardly any of the words. The only words I could make out from here were Holly saying, "No, why?"

Clint believed that he had just witnessed Holly and her boyfriend Drew breaking up. Drew also happened to be Clint's best friend. Deciding that it was not any of his business, he left them to it and didn't give the scene he had just witnessed much thought for the time being. He was unaware that Drew was hunting at his grandmother's property and hence could not have been the man he saw arguing with Holly. The telephone rang and Clint answered – it was his panicked mother asking after Holly. Clint told her what he had just seen taking place outside. Karen Bobo was mortified. She told her son 'Clint. That's not Drew. Get a gun and shoot him.'

Clint's response was underwhelming. Still groggy from sleep, and adamant that the man was in fact Drew, he incredulously asked 'You want me to shoot Drew? And I don't want to call 911 and say "My sister and her boyfriend are breaking up." Probably panicking and not thinking clearly, Karen failed to mention that the man could not be Drew as she knew he was elsewhere, nor did she mention the scream that the neighbor had reported. In any event, she was getting nowhere fast with her son. She hung up on him and called 911 instead. It was 7.55 a.m. by the time Karen called 911. Precious moments were wasted as her call was routed to the incorrect county dispatcher due to the fact that she had called from work and her home was in another county.

Meanwhile back at the Bobo residence, Clint took another look outside. Now he saw Holly walking off into the woods with the man, whom he now realized was wearing camouflage. He later recalled 'The only thing I could see was his right arm, which was hanging down. I saw them up to about where those two trees are, and from that point I never saw them again.' He now started to take the situation more seriously.

He tried to reach Holly on her cell phone but the call rang out. When that did not work Clint attempted to call Drew on his cell phone, but again the call rang out. Clint would later describe the mystery man, who would come to be known as 'Camo Man', as between 5'10" and six foot tall and weighing an approximate 180 to 200 pounds.

At 8.00 a.m. Karen called Clint back. When he told her about the latest development Karen told Clint to call 911 and report it. Arming himself with a loaded pistol, Clint headed outside. He discovered a pool of blood (later confirmed as belonging to Holly) next to his sister's car. He finally called 911.

At some point shortly thereafter police arrived at the Bobo home. So did Karen Bobo and a number of neighbors. It seemed that everybody was just milling about, walking all over the crime scene, potentially compromising evidence and discussing what had happened in those crucial first few hours of the investigation. They are remembered with frustration by those who were present at the scene. Family friend Terri Brumley later recalled 'It seems like it was well over two hours at least before anyone went into the woods. They waited on search dogs to get here and a helicopter.' Karen Bobo later said 'I was begging them to put out road blocks. The bond that Holly and I had - I knew that something was completely, absolutely wrong, but I just couldn't make anybody understand that.'

A widespread hunt then ensued after Holly was abducted, but the searches bore little fruit. Not many clues were left behind. Holly's lunch box was discovered eight miles from the Bobo residence. A distinctive shoeprint from the Croc's brand of foam clogs was also discovered outside Holly's house. It would not be until September 2014 that Holly would finally be found. Unsurprisingly after such a long time, it was not a happy ending to the case. Two ginseng hunters from Benton County discovered what remained of Holly Bobo in some woods near a logging road adjacent to County Corner Road in northern Decatur County, twenty miles from where Holly had been taken. Investigators broke the news at a 10.00 p.m. press conference held at the Decatur County Sheriff's Department. The remains were sent to the Tennessee Bureau of Investigation forensics laboratory in Memphis, which later determined that the remains were indeed that of Holly Bobo. The owner of the property where Holly's partial remains were located said that it was a regular occurrence for people to travel through his property without permission. It was a popular local hunting ground. One of the ginseng hunters spotted a big bucket near the remains, which he emptied. He instantly regretted his decision. Information regarding whatever the man saw has not been released to the general public, however he has stated in interviews that he is haunted by it.

The first arrests in the case came in March 2014, six months prior to the discovery of Holly's remains. To date, details are murky as to the case against the accused and exactly how the investigation came to focus on them. Local brothers Zach and Dylan Adams, along with their friend Jason Autry, stand accused of especially aggravated kidnapping, rape and murder in the first degree. Previously another two brothers, Mark and Jeffrey Pearcy, stood accused of tampering with evidence and accessory after the fact, but the charges against them were later dropped. A sixth man, Shayne Austin, was identified by investigators as a potential person of interest in the case, although formal charges were never filed. Austin committed suicide nearly a year after the first arrests.

Investigators and prosecutors are keeping their cards close to their chests thus far, including details of whether any of the accused had ever met Holly Bobo prior to her murder, or any possible motive for the crime. What is known is that the state is seeking the death penalty in the cases against Autry and the Adams brothers due to the fact that 'The murder was especially heinous, atrocious or cruel in that it involved torture or serious physical abuse beyond that necessary to produce death;' was committed in aid of 'avoiding, interfering with, or preventing a lawful arrest or prosecution;' and was 'knowingly committed, solicited, directed or aided' by the accused (excerpts from court papers).

Zach Adams was the first to be arrested and charged with Holly's murder. This was based on information provided to investigators by his brother Dylan, who told them that he had seen Holly, still alive, at the house he shared with his brother later on the same day that she was taken. He stated that he had gone home to retrieve his truck, and was surprised to find Holly Bobo seated in the living room wearing a pink t-shirt (Holly had indeed been wearing a pink t-shirt when she was last seen) with Jason Autry standing near her. He told investigators Zach was 'wearing camouflage shorts, black cut-off-sleeve t-shirt and a pair of green Crocs.' He further stated that Zach had informed him that 'he had raped Bobo and videotaped it.' No such tape was ever recovered in the search executed on the Adams residence by investigators. They did find a blond hair in a bedroom closet. It is not known if this hair came from Holly.

Jason Autry was the second man to be arrested and charged in connection to the Holly Bobo murder. His especially aggravated kidnapping and first-degree murder charges were laid a month after Zach Adams'. In May 2015 a rape charge was also added. Autry faces the death penalty based purely on Dylan Adams' statement naming him as present with Holly Bobo at the Adams residence on the day of her abduction. No other evidence has surfaced to date.

Investigators offered Shayne Austin an immunity deal for any part he may have played in Holly's murder in exchange for information leading to the recovery of her remains. Police believed that Austin knew where Holly was buried and possibly assisted in the disposal of the body based on the fact that telephone records show that Zach Adams spoke to Austin several times on April 13, 2011, the date of Holly's abduction. The immunity agreement was taken off the table when Austin was unable to tell police what they wanted to know. In revoking the offer the district attorney stated that Austin 'has not been completely truthful, forthcoming and cooperative as to any and all aspects of this investigation.' In April 2014 Austin's attorney filed an injunction request against prosecutors seeking to prevent them from laying charges. In February 2015 Austin committed suicide by hanging himself in a Bartow, Florida hotel room. His attorney pointed the blame squarely at investigators in the Bobo case due to what he termed their 'witch hunt' interrogation tactics, in that their investigation was based largely on hearsay and rumors from unreliable sources instead of actual evidence. The attorney maintains that his client had nothing to do with Holly's murder and that he cooperated with police to the best of his ability.

Investigators also set their sights on Dylan Adams, charging him with evidence tampering and disposal in September 2014. It is not known what specific evidence they were referring to but the charges were later dropped. He was later charged with rape based on a confession he allegedly made to police. Adams' attorney complained that the State has not yet turned over any evidence to him. In May 2015 Adams was further charged with especially aggravated rape, especially aggravated kidnapping and murder in the first degree. Again, any specific evidence against Adams, if any, has not been made known.

In July 2014 investigators charged brothers Jeff and Mark Pearcy with evidence tampering and accessory after the fact after Sandra King (Jeff's former roommate) alleged that two months prior Jeff had shown her a video in which Zach Adams assaults a restrained and crying Holly Bobo, a video that Mark Pearcy supposedly filmed. Working with police, Sandra made a phone call to Jeff in an attempt to trap him into admitting to the existence of said video. While police listened in and recorded the phone call, Sandra said 'That video of Holly - if it had been you, I would have watched it,' to which Jeff replied 'I know.' The Pearcy brothers deny any involvement in the crime and the existence of such a video. Jeff maintains he does not even know Autry or the Adams brothers. Of his comment in the taped phone call, Jeff says that he was not able to hear Sandra clearly and that he thought that she was saying something about his ex-wife (also named Holly). Over twenty phones have been confiscated and searched but no such video has ever been found. All charges against the Pearcy brothers were later dropped. Supposedly District Attorney Matt Stowe, together with the Tennessee Bureau of Investigation, plan to charge more people with additional crimes in connection to the Holly Bobo murder, but he declined to elaborate on who these people or what these charges might be.

In spite of Dylan Adams' initial alleged statements, all three of the accused maintain their innocence in relation to the crimes. Jason Autry said in a media interview in May 2014 'I want to let them know they have an innocent man right here. I'm a drug addict and a thief, but I'm not a killer.' Autry went on to allege that Dylan, who was already serving a jail sentence on unrelated gun charges, made up the story about him and Zach due to bad blood between the brothers and also in the hope of gaining a reduction on his sentence – 'They hate each other's guts and that's a way to get back at him.' Autry also alleges that investigators attempted to coerce him into providing false testimony about Zach Adams.

Dylan's family says that investigators are taking advantage of his low IQ and mental disabilities in order to coerce a fabricated confession that suits their agenda, with a family spokesperson telling reporters that Dylan 'has the mind of a child. They kept him up all night, would not give him anything to eat or drink and finally he said "What do you want me to say?" The family says Dylan can barely read, cannot perform basic tasks like telling the time, getting a false confession out of him would be no more difficult than getting a false confession out of a child.

Similarly, Jeff Pearcy alleges that Sandra King's statements were nothing more than a desperate attempt to leverage a reduction in prison time for her son, who at the time had served fourteen years of a thirty-eight year prison sentence – 'I have been up front and honest about everything. I have willingly given them everything. Take it, I mean, it's there. My heart goes out to the Bobo family. It could have very well been one of my kids. For someone to give them false hope, and that's exactly what's been done to them. But for the justice system to just haul someone in and destroy their whole life, I mean, there's no sense in that at all.'

John Herbison, Autry's attorney, has levelled criticism at the investigation into his client – 'I don't think the state has any case against Jason Autry. If those reports are correct, it means that they're just playing games. They charged him with something less serious in order to keep him locked up, and then when it comes time to answer questions about the charge, they dismiss that and charge him with a more serious charge in circuit court, where he's not entitled to a preliminary hearing.' In response to the prosecution's claim that they only dropped the charges against Mark Pearcy because he was facing unrelated federal charges which took precedence, Herbison said 'If the state is claiming that is the case, the prosecutor is either ill-informed or being disingenuous.'

The prosecution's handling of the case against the accused has been heavily criticized by leading legal experts. It has been marked by the seemingly arbitrary addition and removal of charges at random or as some sort of posturing or game playing on their part, as well as in-fighting between members of the prosecution which has further complicated the case. Indeed, to the outside observer it appears to have been a bumbling affair at several stages of the investigation and prosecution. One might even say that it has descended into the level of farce at times. District Attorney Matt Stowe rose to office in the summer of 2014. He publicly attributed a large part of the rationale for his election as being due to the thus-far bungled murder investigation - 'Voters wanted another set of eyes on this Holly Bobo case. They weren't happy with everything that was coming out of there, and I think that they wanted someone else to take a look and someone else to say "We know what's going on."

They say the wheels of justice turn slowly, but after the prosecution missed several evidence discovery deadlines and appeared to be deliberately and unnecessarily delaying the case, it proved to be too slowly for no-nonsense Judge Creed McGinley, who warned the prosecution 'I am absolutely out of patience with these cases not moving' in ordering that the case against Zach Adams be filed within one week and that evidence discovery take place immediately on December 17, 2014. The prosecution brazenly ignored the judge and his deadlines. Attorneys for the accused filed motions to dismiss, accusing the prosecution of 'silence or stonewalling' on a long list of complaints that also included failure to disclose forensic evidence that the skull found in the woods actually was that of Holly Bobo. Autry's attorney criticized 'It would appear to me if they had a skull with a dental match they would have given that to us right away. It's a little suspicious why we don't have that forensic information.'

In July of 2015, attorneys for the accused finally received access to the state's evidence against their clients. John Herbison filed a subpoena forcing Matt Stowe and TBI director Mark Gwyn to testify at a hearing in relation to the in-house disputes among the TBI and to provide an answer as to why the prosecution was intentionally stalling the case for such an unusually excessive amount of time. Following this December 2015 hearing regarding the bumbling TBI case, the TBI dropped the investigation and severed ties with the district in response to accusations of misconduct made by Matt Stowe. The TBI agreed to resume its investigation after Stowe recused himself and special prosecutor Jennifer Nichols was installed in his place. In response to this turn of events, attorneys for the accused now plan to subpoena Stowe in order to question him about the specifics of his misconduct allegations. Emails written by Wall Kirby, the Executive Director of the Tennessee District Attorney's Conference, exposed some of Stowe's concerns, specifically that the case was moving 'so slowly that the culprits were always one step ahead and that the TBI was leaking information and possibly covering up evidence.'

A hearing set for August 26, 2015 was cancelled so that attorneys for the accused would have a chance to examine evidence belatedly provided by the prosecution. John Herbison speculated that a new date for the hearing might be some time away. The date was eventually set for April 3, 2017, nearly six years after Holly's abduction.

The case has been the subject of intense national media interest, at some times to the detriment of the investigation when inaccuracies have been reported. Holly was first said to have been dragged into the woods by Camo Man. Clint Bobo later stated that this was not the case and that Holly walked into the woods with the man, either willingly or by force. This and other seemingly questionable statements and decisions made by Clint have led to a trial in the court of public opinion, with a popular theory being that Clint killed Holly, or was involved in the murder plot, and has changed his story at times. Questions such as: Why did he just stand by and watch his sister get abducted? Why didn't he listen to his mother? Why did he not pursue the abductor? There has also been a lot of speculation from the public as to Clint's mental capacity. Whitney Duncan took to Twitter on April 17, 2011 to defend Clint, stating 'My cousin Clint, Holly's brother, is NOT a suspect & I'm sick of people saying that he is. He has been cleared for good reason. Shut up.' In turn, police then later clarified that this was not the case. Whilst the investigation was not focusing on Clint, nobody had been 'cleared' as a suspect at that stage.

In actuality, as the sole witness to Holly's abduction, naturally Clint faced some scrutiny. He has taken polygraph tests, been hypnotized, interrogated for more than seventeen hours, handed his cell phone and hard drive over to police and been strip searched (the TBI denied this ever took place). He has received death threats and accusations from people who believe that he killed his sister. Karen Bobo told the media 'They're (people who accuse Clint) warped. In my mind, they're warped.'

The high level of media interest in the case has also led to a plethora of inaccurate tip-offs from well-meaning members of the public, as well as hundreds of leads from dozens of self-professed psychics, that investigators have had to wade through.

One psychic stated 'Bobo's abductor might have a scar on his forehead, or a rash on his elbow, or a bite mark on his hand. He might work from home as a graphic designer and long for the 1950s. His hair might be dark brown, or blonde, or salt and pepper. He might be clean shaven, or he might have a moustache. He might be a Scorpio. He is either scrawny, or of medium build, or stocky and muscular - possibly ex-military. He might own a black leather wallet and his name might contain one or more of the following letters: B, A, J, R, W or M. His last name might be Glenn. Bobo might be, or might have been at one point, in or near a place that has the number seven associated with it. Either an address or a highway number or possibly seven miles from some landmark.' Another psychic believed that the key to finding Holly was hidden within the lyrics of the Neil Diamond song 'September Morn.' Yet another psychic, stated with confidence on April 14, 2011 that Holly would be found alive, that her captor makes a lot of mistakes and would be found within five days. Prominent television psychic profiler Carla Baron of 'Haunting Evidence' offered her services to the Bobo family pro bono, but they declined on the advice of the TBI.

The case has also been cited as an example of Missing White Woman syndrome – a tendency for missing persons cases involving young, white, attractive, upper middle class women (often blondes), to receive a much higher degree of media coverage than that of their counterparts of different ethnicity, social status or gender.

At the time of writing, onlookers eagerly look forward to Jason Autry's and the Adams brothers' day in court.

THE MURDER OF IRA YARMOLENKO

137

DANIELLE SWEET

On a seemingly normal Thursday afternoon on the Catawba River in May of 2008, two jet skiers planned on having a picnic together along the river when they stumbled upon a peculiar sight that would change their lives forever - a car crashed into a stump on the banks of the river along with the horrifying sight of a dead body lying next to it. They quickly alerted authorities and soon discovered that the body was that of a deceased young woman.

This was the tragic fate of Irina "Ira" Yarmolenko, a University of North Carolina college student who had just celebrated her twentieth birthday several days earlier. She was discovered with three items from her car tied around her neck. There was no sign of a struggle or any clear indication of a motive. She was not sexually assaulted or robbed.

Although first responders initially thought her death could have been a suicide, her death was ruled a homicide by asphyxiation. To this day, her murder still garners interest from the public due to the strange yet disturbing circumstances surrounding her death. Add to that the whispers that surround the case about the possibility that her convicted murderer, Mark Carver, might actually be an innocent man. What followed this horrific discovery was an investigation into the crime scene and into her personal life to uncover what happened to Ira.

Ira's early life and college experience

Ira Yarmolenko was born in the Ukraine on May 2nd, 1988 but emigrated to the United States when she was eight, along with her parents and brother Pavel. The family reportedly fled the Ukraine as refugees due to religious persecution. Her parents, both research scientists, were able to find job opportunities in North Carolina.

Ira quickly picked up the language and by all accounts seemed to assimilate well into American culture. She lived in North Carolina for most of her life, spoke with a southern accent and had several personal interests. Like most teenagers, she enjoyed hiking, acting, photography, sports, and music.

She also played the piano and liked listening to bands, such as the Counting Crows. She was also extremely academic. She excelled in math and science while being an active member of her high school poetry team. Ira was especially close to her family. Although she left Chapel Hill for UNC Charlotte, about a 3-hour drive away, she spoke to her mother almost every day. After her death, her mother said to reporters, "I don't think what I'm living is called life anymore."

During her two years in college, she found other interests beyond her required coursework at UNC Charlotte, where she was an undeclared major but had a strong interest in French. She was a photographer for the University Times, her college paper, and occasionally wrote columns and articles for the Niner Online, an online student-run newspaper.

She was also a member of the university's Russian Club as Russian was her first language. Her Russian language classmate described her as, "the kind of girl that always made you feel special, wanted, needed, cared for, and loved. It always seemed like she was always so happy to see you, and would always take at least a second of her time to say hello to you." It was here that she met her roommate Masha, another student from the Ukraine.

Masha and Ira bonded over the fact that they both spoke Russian and came from similar backgrounds. Masha described the day that she found out Ira was murdered when two investigators showed up at the small apartment that she shared with Ira, "It was her student I.D. picture. And I just started screaming. Sorry. Both of our families immigrated here to this country for a better life and sacrificed so much." Like most people close to Ira, Masha was devastated to hear the news of her friend's death.

Most people who knew Ira described her as outgoing. They felt that she would not have been afraid if a stranger had approached her. She was involved on campus and worked at a local coffee shop, Jackson's Java. Years after her death, her picture could still be found on the counter of Jackson's Java. She had a lasting impact on those that knew her. Her brother said, "Everything that she's ever done was to help people."

At UNC Charlotte, she had many close friends and acquaintances who described her as a cheerful and bubbly person, yet still high-achieving. In addition to her job at the coffee shop, Ira also worked as an aid in a computer lab on campus. The week before finals, her roommate Masha and friends threw a party for her 20th birthday.

During this party, her friends reported that Ira ended up cooking for everyone there, despite the fact that party was a celebration in her honor. This was not uncommon for her to do and was just the kind of person she was. Her friends concluded the celebration by visiting an art exhibit. They reported that she was in good spirits and that they parted amicably.

Although it seemed Ira was thriving in her environment at UNC Charlotte, she was in the process of closing her chapter there and beginning a new one at UNC-Chapel Hill, a school a bit closer to home. "Ira indicated she was sad to leave her friends behind at UNCC, but she was looking forward to attending UNC-Chapel Hill in the fall," according to Sgt. Tindall, an investigator in the case.

She had resigned from her positions at the coffee shop and in the computer lab where she had worked during her sophomore year shortly before she was murdered. Her brother Pavel, a then Ph.D. graduate student at Duke said, "She was not sure how she felt about leaving Charlotte. But she was very, very excited about coming to Chapel Hill."

Ira intended on transferring to UNC-Chapel Hill to be closer to her family and to major in public health. The day of her murder, she visited the coffee shop and said goodbye to her friends there and left a gift, a book, for her former boss. She also took several items to the Goodwill to donate and visited her credit union where she deposited some checks before heading to the river about 20 miles away.

The scene of the crime

The Catawba River is over 200 miles long and spans two states. It is located about 20 minutes from Charlotte and is popular among fisherman, boaters and jet skiers. First responders on that fateful day described a perplexing, yet disturbing scene.

The doors on the driver's side of Ira's car were opened, and her body was found just a few feet away. It did not appear she was sexually assaulted or robbed, nor did she have defensive wounds from fighting off her attacker or attackers.

Three ligatures were found around her neck: a nylon ribbon from a bag in her car, a drawstring from the hood of a jacket and a bungee cord. The drawstring was wrapped around her neck. The ribbon was wrapped once around her neck and oddly tied in a bow in the front. Her hair and body were also wet, although she was found on dry ground.

According to Detective Terry during the trial, "Her head was back towards the embankment. Her feet were near the river underneath some brush. Upon closer inspection, she was actually holding some of that brush in her hand. . . ." It was determined that this was the place where she was murdered and that she had not been transferred there.

Investigators began piecing together her movements before arriving at the river banks and determined it was likely that she headed down to the river banks to take pictures, as she was an avid photographer. Her brother Pavel said he "wasn't surprised she would go to such a remote spot. She was adventurous. She once hiked the Stampede Trail in Alaska with friends, searching for an abandoned bus made famous by Jon Krakauer's book Into the Wild."

Her camera was found in the trunk of her car, but there was not any film in it that could yield any clues about her death. Investigators quickly began interviewing people along the river to see if anyone had heard or seen anything out of the ordinary and came across two fishermen who wcrc fishing about 100 yards from where Ira's body and car were discovered.

Mark Carver and Neil Cassada were cousins who grew up in the area and had been fishing in a new spot they had discovered the weekend before. This spot was about 100 yards from where Ira's car and body were discovered. Carver had been excited about the spot. He had returned to it because it did not require him to haul his boat to the river which was difficult for Carver to do since he suffers from carpal tunnel syndrome, a condition that makes his hands extremely weak.

His doctors recommended he not lift anything heavier than five pounds. Cassada also suffered from a heart condition, making it difficult to do anything too physical. Investigators questioned both men who reported that they had not seen Ira or had not heard anything from their fishing spot. They did report hearing a scraping sound that sounded like noise from construction.

They both willingly provided their DNA to investigators and went on their way. With the lack of forensic clues pointing toward any viable suspects, it was not until forensic analysis of the car several months later revealed partial DNA matches for Carver and Cassada that they became the prime suspects for Ira's murder. Mark Carver and Neal Cassada were arrested in December of 2008, seven months after her death and charged with conspiracy and murder. A day before Cassada's the trial began in 2010, Cassada died of a heart attack. Carver has always proclaimed their innocence.

"Simple" life of Mark Carver

Simple is the word often used to describe Mark Carver. "Simple in his routine, simple in his thought process, simple in his desires and wants," defense attorney Brent Ratchford said to reporters. Unlike Ira, Carver is not well-educated and has limitations with writing and reading comprehension, which he has struggled with throughout most of his life.

At an early age, he was placed in special education classes because of these limitations and his relatively low IQ. At 16, he dropped out of school to work in a mill. At the time he was arrested, it was documented that he was taking medication prescribed for schizophrenia.

Carver is also the father of four children from two different marriages. "He lived for his children and family," his sister-in-law Robin Carver said when asked about him. "He didn't really do much of anything else. Fishing and hunting and family, that was about it."

Although his family speaks well of Carver, like most family members often do, he did have prior brushes with the law despite never being convicted of a crime. In 2005, Carver faced a charge of injury to property. Carver purportedly confronted two people he thought were stealing his four-wheeler. The charge was dismissed, and the file no longer exists. A year before Ira's murder, Carver accidentally shot his son. Carver and his son were supposedly wrestling when the gun went off. "It was an accident," his son said. The case was later dismissed and Carver never convicted of a crime.

Cassada also had had his own dealings with the law. In 1995, he was accused of assault and injury to personal property. He reportedly pointed a gun at someone. But the charges were dismissed and the details remain unclear.

His family insists that he had nothing to do with Ira's murder and that the stress of the trial for a crime he did not commit ultimately led to his death. Kaye Cassada, Neal Cassada's wife said "After 37 years of loving that man and being married to that man, I know he is not capable of hurting anybody. He would have died to help somebody." Charges against Cassada were dropped, a common proceeding with deceased suspects. His family attended the hearing and his son Shannon Cassada said, "We want everybody to hear that he was an innocent man."

Carver also maintains his own innocence, stating "they said that they had ... my DNA and Neal's DNA in the car. I know that's a lie because Neal left, and they couldn't have gotten no DNA because I wasn't down there. I didn't go around it. I didn't go around the car. You know what I'm saying?" He also said he didn't think Cassada would commit such a crime because "He's got four young'uns himself."

Although lie detector tests are not reliable enough to be used in court, during the initial investigation Cassada took a polygraph test, which he passed. Because he passed, investigators did not give Carver one. Carver has been very vocal about his willingness to also take a polygraph test.

Touch DNA

During the investigation and trial, Carver never wavered in proclaiming his innocence and said this to Ira's family "I never seen her that day. If I'd knowed she was up there, I would have went up there and helped her. They could have easily come down and killed me just like they did her."

His trial began in 2010. Before the trial, Carver was offered a surprising plea deal from the prosecution: 4-8 years in prison if he pleaded guilty to second degree murder. Had he taken this deal and pled guilty to murder he could be out of prison and with his family. His attorney said, "I have never gotten such a low offer. And to me that spoke volumes about the case." Carver turned down this offer and prosecutors moved forward with the case.

Prosecutors argued that the two men killed Ira because she witnessed or photographed something they did not want her to see. As a result, they strangled her and pushed her car on the embankment where their DNA was transferred to the car. Their intention was to sink the car in the water, but it hit a stump where it stayed until it was finally discovered by the jet skiers. They then returned to their fishing spot until they were questioned by police.

Prosecutors relied on a relatively new forensic technique at the time known as "touch DNA." Unlike previous methods, touch DNA uses smaller amounts of DNA, such as skin cells transferred to a person or object when they come into contact with someone. But touch DNA is not as reliable as other DNA methods requiring blood or saliva because it is difficult to determine the origin of these cells. For instance, skin cells can be transferred indirectly by a third party or carrier.

For example, a man in California was falsely imprisoned because his DNA was found on a murder victim. It was determined that it was impossible that he was a killer because he had a solid alibi. At the time of the murder, he was unconscious in a hospital due to extreme intoxication.

Prosecutors then discovered that the same paramedic who treated him for intoxication was a first responder at the murder scene. The DNA from the intoxicated man was presumably transferred to the victim by the paramedic. This case set a precedent about the reliability of touch DNA and is cited by Carver's advocates for innocence as a possibility as to why Carver's and Cassada's DNA was found on Ira's car.

Despite this interesting theory, it was not presented by the defense in Carver's trial and the jury found him guilty of murder. He was sentenced to and is currently serving life in prison. Carver's advocates argue that the car and crime scene was not preserved, and that Carver and Cassada's DNA could have been transferred by officers or other people near the crime scene. Many officers, the jet skiers, first responders were all present at the crime scene and could have all inadvertently transferred the DNA to the car.

Several other inconsistencies exist in the prosecution's case. Carvers DNA was not found on her body nor on the trunk of the car where he and Cassada would have pushed it into the river bank according to prosecutors. Carvers DNA did not match a third DNA profile found on the bungee cord and the only DNA found under Ira's fingernails was her own.

His attorney and advocates also argue that the two men couldn't have physically pushed the car into the river bank due to Carver's carpal tunnel and Cassada's heart condition. Cassada supposedly got winded just walking. In 2013, Carver's attorneys filed an appeal on his behalf, but the appeals court determined "no error in the defendant's trial" occurred, meaning his conviction of life in prison would be upheld. But this did not deter his advocates from trying to prove Carver did not receive a fair defense during his trial.

Earlier this year, a judge granted the request of the North Carolina Actual Innocence Project, attorneys who have become interested in Carver case who believe Carver is wrongfully imprisoned, to see DNA reports that were never shared with Carvers defense team, along with further DNA testing.

They argue that Carver did not receive a proper defense as his lawyers did not call any witnesses or DNA experts to the stand and address the DNA evidence, and that the DNA evidence is not compelling enough beyond a reasonable doubt to warrant a life sentence for Carver. It is the only evidence linking Carver to the crime. Only time will determine the final outcomes of Carver's appeals as the evidentiary hearing has been postponed. Legal proceedings could take several years.

Other suspects

If Carver and Cassada's DNA was indeed transferred by a third party and they did not kill Ira, then who did? There was no one in her life that seemed to have any motive. Besides these two men, there was only one other suspect in her murder investigation. Nine months after the murder, Christopher Lemont Cooper wrote a letter to News anchor Erica Bryant to "confess a sin," that he and several other accomplices had killed Ira.

He said he drove a van full of friends that were all high and needed money for drugs. He said he was unable to sleep "because of what we did to that young woman." And wished to meet with the reporter. The TV station did not publish the letter and turned it over to investigators where they took the letter very seriously and launched an investigation with the North Carolina State Bureau of Investigations.

Police and investigators visited Cooper, where he was in jail on charges of rape, assault by strangulation, and for being delinquent in child support. He reportedly refused to cooperate with investigators, but they ultimately ruled him out as a suspect concluding that several of the accomplices he named were incarcerated at the time of the murder. They also cleared the other accomplices named in Cooper's letter and continued building their case against Carver and Cassada.

Free Mark Carver

Free Mark Carver is one of the prominent websites advocating for the release of Carver. They believe he is innocent or at the very least did not receive a proper defense in his trial. The website is run by a former newspaper journalist who now works in the fashion industry. She had no ties to the case or families and became intrigued with the case in 2011 after its details aired on Dateline NBC and through other online news articles.

One of the major theories from Carver's advocates presented on the website is that Ira was not murdered and in fact committed suicide by placing the ligatures around her neck herself. They claim that Ira was not the cheerful person described by her friends and loved ones and that she had battled depression.

Her boyfriend had broken up with her shortly before her murder and her poetry was sometimes dark and melancholy. The website alludes to accounts from unnamed people who claim that Ira had attempted suicide when she was younger and had seen a therapist at UNC Charlotte. The website does not provide sources and only mentions them as letters to the author.

Although this theory may be offensive to those who loved Ira and describe her as a happy and vibrant young woman, it has been addressed by pathologists who have dismissed this theory saying "For this to have been anything but a homicide, i.e., this was a suicide, this victim would have to tie three ligatures around her neck tightly and before death get into this position while that's going on and her legs underneath the brush given that position and I just feel like that was not consistent with what we are seeing. . . . Yes, and another thing that this illustrates a little bit better also is the presence of particular matter, soil and grass on her skirt as well. So that's another thing that would have had to happen. If this was a suicide she would have had to do all this stuff by herself. It is just not consistent with that theory."

Her brother Pavel, who has since completed his Ph.D. in biomedical engineering and continues to conduct research at a pediatric hospital, said he has read some of the internet theories about his sister's death, but they are "not grounded in reality." He asserts that his sister never attempted suicide and there was no indication she was depressed. Nevertheless, the fact remains that a lively, young woman lost her life just days after her 20th birthday.

Memorials

We may never know what really happened to Ira or why someone chose to take her life but it is clear that she touched many people who strive to keep her memory alive. The jet skiers who found her body, Dennis Lovelace and Brenda Pierce, placed a memorial cross where they found her car. The changing levels of the Catawba river sometimes covers part of the cross, but it is still visible to visitors.

A memorial bench as far as Alaska, where Ira spent a summer waitressing, also bears her name. "A Kansas City based artist Shane Blindt designed and installed this bench at the request of many co-workers whose lives were touched with Ira's presence during the 2007 McKinley Village Lodge summer season. Lettering on the memorial was hand drawn with pen showing the elegance and beauty of Ira's outward expressions contrasted with a raw and rugged placement into the world she left behind." It is maintained by locals there.

Her high school poetry team in Chapel Hill renamed the group The Sacrificial Poets in her honor.

What Time Devours is a book written by her former professor at UNC Charlotte who dedicated his book to her memory. He directed a campus production, which Ira was a part of the previous year before she was murdered. He also included a line from her poetry and her picture in the dedication of the book.

The controversy around her murder continues to intrigue people and several websites and pages are dedicated to outlining the details of the case. Ira's murder has been featured on Dateline and 20/20. She continues to captivate an almost cult following, and many people are still tirelessly working to prove that Carver is innocent and did not receive a fair trial. If this is the case, it means that justice has not been served for Ira and her family. But one thing is for sure, the memory of Ira Yarmolenko will continue to live on with her family, friends, and strangers that have been touched by her story.

FINDING JENNIFER : THE DISAPPEARANCE OF JENNIFER KESSE

MARY DANIELLE TAYLOR

The unsolved disappearance of Jennifer Kesse from her Orlando, Florida condo in the early hours of January 23, 2006, garnered widespread attention from the local and national media alike, leading to large-scale search parties conducted by the Orlando Police Department and FBI. However, despite the fact that Jennifer Kesse disappeared over ten years ago in the parking lot of her apartment complex, investigators are no closer to solving the case.

Jennifer Kesse, a finance manager for a Florida property and vacation company, had left her recently purchased condo in Orlando, Florida to begin her morning commute to work. However, Jennifer would never make it into work that morning, and her family and friends would never hear from her again. Read on to learn more about who Jennifer Kesse was, about the circumstances of her disappearance, and the local and national reaction to her missing persons case.

Early Life

Jennifer Kesse, a graduate of Vivian Gaither High School in Tampa, Florida, had graduated with a degree in finance from the University of Central Florida, located in Orlando, Florida, in 2003, where she also served as a member of the Alpha Delta Pi sorority. Following her graduation from college, Jennifer began working at the Central Florida Investments Timeshare Company as a finance manager.

Shortly before the date of her disappearance, Jennifer and her current boyfriend had visited Saint Croix, in the U.S. Virgin Islands, for a vacation. After returning home from the Virgin Islands by plane, Jennifer drove directly from her boyfriend's house in South Florida to her job in Ocoee, Florida for a full day of work. Jennifer would return home to her newly-purchased condo in Orlando that evening, the very same evening of her disappearance.

Night of Her Disappearance

Jennifer was last seen leaving the Westgate Resorts office of the Central Florida Investments Timeshare Company on the night of

January 23, 2006 in Ocoee, Florida, after returning home from her vacation in Saint Croix, in the U.S. Virgin Islands, with her boyfriend. Several close friends and members of her family received calls from Jennifer that night, and the last call that she made before her disappearance was to her boyfriend shortly before 10:00pm.

Jennifer typically called or texted her boyfriend during her morning commute to work to wish him good morning; however, he became concerned on the morning of January 24th when he did not receive a message from her. When he attempted to call Jennifer that morning, his call was sent directly to voicemail. Because Jennifer had previously told him that she had an early-morning meeting at work, he assumed that she was busy and would call him once she received his voicemail. He continued his day at work until receiving a call from Jennifer's parents later that day informing him that she had never made it to work.

When Jennifer did not show up to work or contact her direct supervisor, a coworker contacted Jennifer's parents to express concern and see if they had heard from her. Jennifer was supposed to attend a very important work meeting with her higher-ups that morning, and it was extremely unlike her to fail to show up with calling ahead. Upon receiving the call from Jennifer's office, her parents immediately jumped into action. Her father, Drew Kesse, said "We were calling hospitals, calling jails, calling her friends, asking them to call places, calling Rob, and he tried calling her and she did not answer."

Her parents soon jumped into their car and made the two-hour drive to Jennifer's condo in Orlando, Florida from their home in Tampa. While driving, her parents contact her condo management office at *Mosaic Apartments*, located on the 3700 block Convoy Road in Orlando, and requested that the manager stop by her condo to check on her. He reported that she was not home, that her condo was in great condition, and that her car was not in the parking lot.

In addition, once her parents arrived in Orlando and entered their daughter's condo, they did not notice anything out of place or any signs of a struggle. Furthermore, they noticed that Jennifer's clothes were laid out on her bed and that a wet towel was present in the restroom, leading them to believe that Jennifer was at home that morning. Her father Drew later said, "We actually found two or three outfits laid out on her bed she was picking. Showered, shower was still damp. Her towel was still damp. Her work stuff was not there. So we knew that, OK, she got ready for work."

The parents quickly contacted the Orlando police department to report her as missing. Family members began passing out flyers that evening and reaching out to local media organizations, while the local police department began organizing a search party.

A local television reporter and friend of Jennifer's, Scott Thuman, described the family's actions like this: "I made sure they were on every TV station every single night as long as we could keep that alive. They did the networks, they did radio shows. They did every newspaper interview they could." An investigative reporter who covered the case would later say, "It was hard to go anywhere without seeing her face and her picture and also the information on her vehicle."

Timeline

January 23, 2006

Early Morning – Leaves her boyfriend's home in Central Florida to head directly to her office at Westgate Resorts for a full day at work. Jennifer and her boyfriend had just returned from a trip to Saint Croix, U.S. Virgin Islands.

6:00pm – Jennifer leaves her office at Westgate Resorts and drives to her condo complex in Orlando, Florida. She unpacks her clothes and contacts several family members to let them know that she has returned home from vacation safely.

10:00pm – Jennifer calls her boyfriend and speaks with him for several minutes before saying goodnight. Jennifer's boyfriend is the last known person to speak with her before her disappearance.

January 24, 2006

7:30am – Police believe that Jennifer was abducted sometime around 7:30am to 8:00am on the morning of the 24th. She was likely taken either while walking through the parking lot towards her car or while entering her vehicle.

8:30am – Jennifer's boyfriend calls her, but the call is sent directly to voicemail. Jennifer typically calls her boyfriend during her morning commute to say good morning and chat. He assumes that she is busy with an early-morning meeting that they had previously discussed.

11:00am – Jennifer's coworkers, concerned that she uncharacteristically did not show up to work and had missed a very important meeting, called her parents to see if Jennifer is okay. Both her parents and coworkers realize that something is wrong.

11:15am – Jennifer's parents immediately begin the two-hour drive to Jennifer's condo in Orlando from their home in Tampa. Her parents contact her condo's management office and request that they enter her condo to check on her. He reports that nothing is out of the ordinary and that her car is gone.

12:00pm – Jennifer's brother, who lives locally, arrives at her condo complex and begins looking for her. Unbeknownst to anyone at the time, a surveillance camera at an apartment complex 1 mile down the road from her own condo shows an unidentifiable man parking Jennifer's car. The video shows the suspect parking the car, and sitting in it for approximately 30 seconds before exiting the car and walking away from the complex. Unfortunately for investigators, the suspect's face was obscured by a fencing post and neither the local police department nor the FBI were able to produce a useable shot of the suspect's face.

1:00pm – Jennifer's parents arrive in Orlando and immediately enter her condo. They notice that her shower is covered with water and that her towel is still wet. They also see that her work clothes are laid out on her unmade bed, that her makeup and hairdryer are lying out on her bathroom sink, and that her pajamas are piled on the restroom floor. Police theorize that Jennifer may have had a fight with her boyfriend and left her apartment to cool off. They preach patience to the parents.

5:00pm – Jennifer's close family and friends begin passing out missing persons flyers to local passerby. The police respond by sending a detective to her condo to gather information and investigate her disappearance. Police begin to question her family and friends, and begin to organize a search party.

January 26, 2006

8:10am – After seeing a report on Jennifer's disappearance on the local news, a resident at a local apartment complex calls the Orlando Police Department to report that her car has been parked in their complex for the last two days. Police arrive at the complex to verify this report, and quickly haul the car away to local police facilities for a forensic analysis. Police are finally able to identify and locate security footage showing an unidentified person parking Jennifer's car and leaving the complex by foot. This footage would lead investigators to determine that Jennifer may have been abducted.

Investigation

Jennifer's parents, as well as the initial investigators who looked into her case, noticed that Jennifer's apartment showed no signs of forced entry, her condo door was locked, and there were no signs of a struggle. Furthermore, because Jennifer's work clothes were laid out neatly and there was evidence that she had recently showered, investigators theorized that she had gotten ready for work the morning of her disappearance and had left her condo to begin her morning commute. The also assert that Jennifer likely left her apartment and was abducted either during the walk to her car or as she was entering the vehicle.

Two days after Jennifer's disappearance on January 26th, her 2004 black Chevy Malibu was located at the *Huntington on the Green* apartment complex, located at Americana Ave. and Texas, a little over a mile away from her own condo. While the apartment complex her car was parked at did have several security cameras, covering both her car and the exit to the apartment complex itself, the videos offered limited clues to her disappearance.

The video showed a "person of interest" who dropped off her car at noon the day of her disappearance; however, the best shots from the video were rendered useless since fencing from the apartment complex concealed the face of the unidentified man in three separate frames. The suspect was seen wearing an all-white uniform, leading some close to the case to believe that the suspect was a painter or other type of manual laborer.

Beau Zimmer, an investigative reporter who followed Jennifer Kesse's disappearance, described the video like this: "There's two different angles, all surrounding the pool area. But it's very, very blurry and it's hard to see. But you can see someone pulling Jennifer's car into that visitor's parking lot. They wait inside the car for a number of seconds before they get out and look around, and then walk out of frame of the picture. But the next shot of the video was what everyone thought would be so helpful. The next shot was of a person that was walking back and forth along the fence line."

However, he noted, "Every frame of the video, the person is obscured by a post and so you never see the person's face." Zimmer would later remark, "It has got to be the most frustrating thing for detectives, the most frustrating thing for the Kesse family, because for just one split second, later or earlier, you would have seen that individual's face and you would have had a better idea of what happened to Jennifer."

When investigators shared footage from the video with Jennifer's family and friends, they were unable to identify the man in question. A Fox News reporter would later say in a televised retrospective segment on the case that the obscured image made the man the "luckiest person of interest ever."

Both the FBI and NASA were called in to conduct advanced video analyses of the footage to provide more clues on the stalled case. The FBI determined that the person was roughly 5'3" to 5'5" tall, but could not offer definitive proof of the suspect's gender. Despite NASA's digital enhancement of the video, they were not able to provide any additional information that could help the case.

Despite the dead-end that the surveillance video represented, investigators were able to put together several pieces of the puzzle. Since all of Jennifer's valuables were found in her car, parked a mile down the street in a different apartment complex, they were able to determine that robbery was not a primary motive in her disappearance. In addition, a police dog was able to track a scent a full mile from her parked car back to her condo complex, leading investigators to theorize that the unidentified suspect returned to her complex directly after disposing of her car. However, police were unable to locate any helpful evidence along the route walked by the suspect.

After conducted a search and forensic analysis of her vehicle, investigators identified two pieces of evidence: a latent fingerprint from an unidentified individual and a small strand of DNA. Given the lack of evidence found in the car, coupled with the lack of clothing fibers, hair strands, and DNA, the police believe that the car was thoroughly wiped down in an attempt to remove incriminating evidence. The investigative reporter assigned to the case, Beau Zimmer, would say, "There was maybe one print and detectives think that it was maybe wiped down, and that this was an intentional act to not only hide this vehicle, but also to hide any evidence of who may have driven it."

Despite the lack of evidence found in her car, investigators did notice that several items were missing. They were unable to located her cell phone, keys, purse, clothes, briefcase, or iPod. While police are often able to track a missing person's cell phone or bank accounts for clues, her bank account was never accessed by her captors and her cell phone remained turned off with the battery removed.

Investigators quickly compiled a list of potential suspects after questioning her friends and family for clues. Her current boyfriend was questioned and quickly eliminated from the list of suspects after providing a valid alibi. In addition, Jennifer's ex-boyfriend and one of her coworkers, who had romantic feelings for Jennifer and had sought a relationship with her in the past, were interviewed by the police.

One the of the most interesting factors in Jennifer's disappearance was the fact that her condo complex was undergoing major construction at the time of her disappearance. Many of the workers, some who were undocumented immigrants, were living in the complex while it was undergoing construction. Jennifer had mentioned her discomfort with some of the workers to her family on multiple occasions, claiming that they harassed and catcalled her regularly. Jennifer's parents have also stated on multiple occasions that they believe she may have been a victim of human trafficking.

In May 2007, the CEO of Central Florida Investments Timeshare Company, David Siegel, offered a $1 million reward for information that led to her being found alive; however, the reward was never claimed. A $5,000 reward for information on her disappearance, offered by the Central Florida Crime line, remains active today.

Suspects

Ex-boyfriend

Jennifer had recently broken up with a previous boyfriend, and he was reportedly very angry about the breakup and the fact that Jennifer was now dating another man. Beau Zimmer would report that Jennifer's ex-boyfriend became incredibly angry after finding out that she was travelling to Saint Croix with Rob, saying "The night before or sometime before, he had been out drinking and gotten drunk and apparently he was upset that he was not the one that was with Jennifer.

Zimmer would later remark that the ex-boyfriend was cleared by the police, saying "They talked with him several times, and while police say he is not a suspect in the case, certainly you get the feeling from others that he should be talked to a little bit more."

Current Boyfriend

Jennifer's boyfriend, Rob, was initially considered a suspect in her disappearance. The couple had just returned from a vacation in Saint Croix, in the U.S. Virgin Islands, and Rob was the last person who had spoken with Jennifer the night before her disappearance. Police soon interviewed Rob to learn more about his relationship with Jennifer and to ascertain his whereabouts the morning of her disappearance.

However, Rob was quickly discounted as a suspected. Rob had an airtight alibi; he was more than 200 miles away when Jennifer was abducted, at his home in Fort Lauderdale, Florida. Investigative journalist Beau Zimmer says, "The police said that between his phone records and the fact that he was in South Florida, we don't believe that he was involved."

The police department's belief in Rob's innocence is shared by Jennifer's family. He was fully cooperative with the police department and FBI's investigation and willingly provided a DNA sample twice. Jennifer's father, Drew Kesse, said "Rob has been put over the coals, Rob has been polygraphed three of four times, Rob has been interviewed probably over a dozen times."

Coworker

Both Jennifer's family, friends, and coworkers reported that Jennifer had recently turned down a coworker who was hitting on her and attempting to strike up a romantic relationship. Jennifer's mom, Joyce, said that the coworker was married and was refusing to accept Jennifer's decision not to date him, both because he was married and because she did not date people she worked with. Joyce later said, "Jennifer arranged to meet him in the cafeteria at work so that once and for all she could tell him, 'Leave me alone, I am never going to date you. And besides, I don't date married men.'"

The police department did question Jennifer's coworker and eventually eliminated him from the list of suspects. However, Joyce said "We feel it should have been consistent to keep the pressure on that individual."

Construction Workers

Jennifer, who had just purchased and moved into her newly renovated condo two months before her disappearance, had repeatedly expressed concern about construction workers in her complex. The complex, which was undergoing extensive renovations at the time, was housing undocumented immigrants working on the consecution projects, at the time of her disappearance. Beau Zimmer has stated, "Jennifer told some of her friends that she felt really uncomfortable around some of these guys. Apparently there may have been some cat calls and things like that."

Jennifer's parents have also stated that she may have been abducted by a construction worker, with her mother saying, "I can't help wonder if someone was stalking her from afar that she didn't even know. Could there have been someone watching her comings and goings?"

The local police department did question many of the construction workers who were working at her condo complex at the time of her disappearance; however, no leads would develop from this line of questioning. Zimmer would say, "The police tried to talk to as many of the workers that would have been there when Jennifer disappeared, but they acknowledge that they may have missed some people."

Sex Traffickers

Drew Kesse has claimed that it is well-known that there was an active sex trafficking ring in the Orlando area at the time of Jennifer's disappearance, which her parents think may be linked to her abduction. Jennifer's father, Drew Kesse, has stated "My gut feeling to this day, honestly, I truly believe she was trafficked." His sentiment was echoed by Jennifer's close friend and local television reporter Scott Thuman, was said "It would make sense on a lot of levels, as unfortunate as it is."

Reaction

The disappearance of Jennifer Kesse led to nationwide outrage and attention, with coverage in the local, state, national, and international media. At the behest of Orlando Police Department chief Val Demings, the FBI took over control of the case on June 10, 2010 and remains in-charge of her missing persons case to this day. She remains on the FBI's Missing List and they continue to search for her and react to current leads, with the most recent search taking place in February 2014. She is also still considered still missing by the Orlando Police Department, Interpol, and the Orange County, Florida Police Department.

In reaction to Jennifer's disappearance and the investigation into her disappearance. The Florida House of Representatives passed Senate Bill 502, entitled "The Jennifer Kesse and Tiffany Sessions Missing Persons Act," by unanimous vote on May 2, 2008. This bill changed the way that missing persons cases are handled in the state of Florida, instituting reforms such as allowing the Florida Department of Law Enforcement to provide assistance in missing persons cases involving adults. Prior to the passage of this law, the FDLE was limited in its ability to provide assistance in cases involving the disappearance or abduction of adults aged 26 or older.

JODI HUISENTRUIT

CARLA PERRY

Jodi Sue Huisentruit was a news anchor for KIMT, a station based in Mason City, Iowa. On June 27th, 1995, she called the station and told her co-worker that she was on her way to work after she overslept.

It would be the last time anyone heard from her.

There were signs of a struggle outside of her apartment indicating that she had been abducted. She would disappear without a trace. Numerous rumors and "persons of interest" have emerged but no official suspect has ever been named.

Over twenty years later, the question still remains.

What happened to Jodi Huisentruit?

EARLY LIFE

Jodi was born in Long Prairie, Minnesota, the youngest daughter of Maurice Huisentruit and Imogene "Jane" Huisentruit. Her father would pass away at age sixty-two of colon cancer. Jodi was only fourteen at the time.

Jodi was an excellent student who also excelled at golf. She would lead her high school team to victory in the state Class A tournament in 1985 and 1986. After high school, she would attend St. Cloud State University where she majored in TV Broadcasting and Speech Communication.

After graduating college, she worked for Northwest Airlines as a stewardess until she landed her first broadcasting gig at KGAN in Cedar Rapids, Iowa. She then briefly returned to Minnesota to work at KSAX before relocating to Iowa for a job at KIMT.

Jodi was well-liked at the station and immediately became a hit with her viewers who liked the infectious enthusiasm of the sunny blonde. She was petite, blonde and had a made for television smile.

Family members, however, would often worry about Jodi as they perceived her as a bit naïve.

"She would befriend anyone," investigative reporter Steve Powell said. "It was part of her nature and that is what made her a popular fixture at the station. In some of her family home videos, you can see the playfulness of her nature. She was outgoing and bubbly. Not the type of person who made enemies."

"I hired Jodi," said Doug Merbach, former news director of KIMT. "I brought her to Mason City. Could there have been something we could have warned her about and talked to her about? I don't know. What do you think happened? I've been asked that so many times. I feel as ignorant as the next person. I just don't know. I don't want to point fingers at anybody without looking inside the investigation and opening up those books. I don't know. I think it had to be somebody who knew her. I think it had to be somebody who had an emotional response to something Jodi said or did that caused them to do that. I don't think it was random - I don't think it was planned. I think it was planned to a certain extent - but not days and weeks ahead of time."

"She had so much enthusiasm," her best friend at the station, Robin Woflram said. "Every day was a gift and treated as something to explore. Sometimes occasionally she would call, I mean this girl got up at 3 am, and she said 'What are you doing after work?' It's like 10:30 pm and I'd tell her that I'm going home and going to bed. She'd say, 'Oh, Robin, there's plenty of time to sleep. Life is for the living.' And she embraced every single moment."

"It's sometimes difficult to get close - especially women - in this industry because you're always looking over your shoulder and wondering if someone is coming up behind me. I'll never forget the first day she walked in and her laugh. She'll always be remembered for that. She's fun and spunky. I think I'll like her. She's got zest for living."

JODI IS MISSING

Huisentruit would play in a golf tournament the day before she disappeared. She then went to the home of John Vansice and according to him, they watched a videotape of her birthday party that he had arranged for her.

On June 27th, 1995, KIMT producer Amy Kuns noticed that Jodi still had not reported for work. She called her at the apartment and explained that she had overslept.

"I'm on my way," Jodi said.

Two hours later, Jodi still had not arrived at the station.

Kuns would substitute for her on her morning show Daybreak.

An hour later, she would call the Mason City police.

"It became known only after that Jodi wasn't always punctual," Powell said. "A lot of her co-workers covered for her because they didn't want her to get in trouble with the brass at the station. So, her arriving late wasn't that much of an unusual occurrence. Not showing up at all certainly was, however, and they called for the police to do a welfare check."

Police would arrive at Jodi's apartment and find her red Mazda Miata still parked in the apartment lot. There was evidence suggesting that there had been a struggle near her car.

Jodi's keys were stuck in the driver side door, broken in half. Her blow dryer, jewelry, and red high heels were strewn about in the parking lot.

The top of her convertible was dented. Blood and tissue was splattered on the driver side mirror. Skid marks on the pavement suggested that she had been dragged to a waiting vehicle."

"The scene suggested that she had been grabbed while putting her keys in the car door," Powell said. "She was in a rush, having overslept for whatever reason. Was probably going to make herself up on the way to the station when someone rushed up behind her."

There was a palm print left behind on her car which police were never able to identify.

MORNING SCREAMS

Police would inquire with neighbors and found three tenants who stated that they heard screams in the early morning hours. Another neighbor reported seeing a white van with lights on parked nearby Jodi's vehicle.

Three months after her disappearance, Jodi's family would hire private investigators from McCarthy and Associates (MAIS) in Minneapolis who then worked in tandem with another private investigator, Doug Jasa.

"A lot of things struck me about the case," Jasa said. "I still remember all of the cards they found in Jodi's apartment. They were birthday cards. I think there were 50 of them and we're reading through them - reading through them. People had written very nice notes in the birthday cards. We went door to door in the apartment complex - talking with different residences about what they heard. One lady remembers specifically looking at her clock when she heard the scream."

Her family held out hope throughout the harrowing ordeal.

"I couldn't have had a better kid sister," Jodi's older sister Joanne Nathe said. "She tried to motivate me. What are your goals? That makes me stronger. It's a nightmare...not knowing where she is. We were hoping to find her in the first few months."

Neither the police nor the private investigators would come up with any evidence. All they had were more questions.

Questions that would forever remain unanswered.

"What caused her to sleep in that day," Officer Terrance Prochaska with Mason City Police Department asked. "What caused her to answer the phone and rush into work? What was she doing the night before? We all want to know the fine details. We know where she was at. She was golfing. She had driven home and made a phone call to her friend. Those are facts. But its' that gray area in between that we don't understand."

Rumors would plague the investigation as numerous false hopes and bizarre allegations were made. Mason City had a growing drug problem and some speculated that Jodi was working on a story to expose drug dealers. This was an outlandish claim considering that Jodi was not an investigative reporter and was not trained for that discipline. KIMT was a call-in television station. They got their news from the wires and reported it after some fact-checking. Another unfounded rumor came from a disgruntled female police officer who claimed that two of her fellow officers were responsible for Jodi's disappearance. Again, these were uncorroborated allegations and the officer spreading the rumors was terminated.

The community at large would get involved and in May of 1996, over one hundred volunteers searched the area of Cerro Gordo County. They would leave flags in the ground to mark anything they found to be suspicious. Authorities would then comb through the area but no further evidence was ever found.

Over one thousand interviews were conducted after her disappearance. Not one single suspect ever emerged.

Police initially turned their attention to the last person to have seen Jodi alive.

John Vansice.

Vansice was a lifelong Iowa native and lived in Newton where he was married with two children. He divorced in the early 1990s and moved to the Key Apartments in Mason City where he would befriend Jodi.

Jodi would reportedly spend a lot of time with the fifty-year-old Vansice. He was more than twenty years her senior and seemed to be "obsessed" with her. He threw around more money than his listed occupation (corn seeder) would suggest he could afford as he purchased a $26,000 boat in 1995 which he named "Jodi".

Jodi's purchase of the Mazda Miata seemed fishy as well as the car was more expensive than her meager salary as a broadcaster would allow.

STRANGER OR STALKER?

"I was the last to see her alive," Vansice said as he approached law enforcement officers investigating Jodi's apartment. He told police of what happened the night before, that Jodi was at his apartment watching a birthday video.

Vansice had taken special care in throwing Jodi a birthday party. He had printed out the invites himself, making sure his name was printed on the bottom with the words "a party given by John Vansice and friends."

Joann described Vansice as being "fixated" on her sister but stated that Jodi never mentioned anything about him during their conversations. She did mention Vansice in conversations with her mother and alluded to the fact that he may be developing a romantic interest in her. She also stated that she felt "uncomfortable" during a recent breakfast she had with Vansice.

Joann would describe a meeting she had with Vansice in which she thought his behavior was "cold" and "unfriendly." She asked Vansice if Jodi ever mentioned their Dad to him and he abruptly ended their conversation.

During his public appearances, Vansice seemed calm in relaying his support for Jodi's return.

Too calm.

"We're all praying and hoping that she's okay," Vansice said. "We just have to keep praying and keep hoping and I'll think she'll come back. I really do."

"I liked Jodi so much I named my boat after her," Vansice said when asked by a reporter why he named his boat after her. "She was such a big part of my life and she just made me feel so good."

Jodi's friend, Tammy Baker, once asked Jodi point blank if she was involved with Vansice.

"Absolutely not," Jodi said.

"Vansice was questioned by police but ruled out as he passed the lie detector tests," Powell said. "But any sociopath can pass a lie detector test. Vansice should have been suspect number one on the basis of telling the police that he 'was the last one to see her alive.' Making a statement like that, with no dead body found, is a revealing disclosure."

Most people close to the case believe that Vansice is involved but never directly say his name as if they are afraid.

"It is a head scratcher as to why the police didn't come at him harder," Powell said. "It was almost as if there was a veil of secrecy over his relationship with Jodi and what it exactly entailed. I believe that it may have been in part to protect Jodi's reputation. She was an All-American girl, church-raised and church-going. But the question had to be asked of what her relationship with Vansice exactly was or more specifically, what did he have in mind? Did he want to be her older sugar daddy? He bought her gifts, gave her birthday parties, making deposits in the account so to speak. But when he finally came to collect did she rebuff his advances and spur him to murderous anger?"

"What is certain is that he was her neighbor and they would hang out a lot. When they looked into her apartment they would find four cans of sixteen-ounce beers. No way the petite Jodi could handle that and then head off to work. The toilet seat was up. The other thing missing from her apartment was her personal notebook. Most sexual predators wouldn't steal something like that. But again, hindsight is 20/20 and they should have made a beeline for Vansice's boat the moment they found out that he named his boat after a woman whom he supposedly had a platonic relationship with."

THE DEATH OF A FRIEND

Three months prior to her disappearance, Jodi suffered the loss of a close friend named Billy Pruin. Pruin had just proposed to his girlfriend Gretchen Tusler and two days later he drove to Mason City to pick up a new tractor he had purchased. The next day, a friend went to his farmhouse and saw that his front door was ajar with the keys in the outside lock. He called out for his friend, received no answer, then he left.

No one had heard from Billy and then his mother went to his house to check on him. She would find him laying in a pool of blood, he had been shot in the chest.

Investigators listed his death as a suicide but later changed it to "undetermined".

His friends, Jodi included, could not believe that the jovial Billy committed suicide. He had just proposed to his girlfriend and bought a new tractor for a business. He had no reason to kill himself.

When Jodi disappeared, there was conjecture that the two deaths could be related.

His fiancee, Gretchen, was questioned after his death and stated that he often appeared "afraid of something" for weeks before his death.

Jodi voiced the same concerns prior to her disappearance. She written one of her best friends, Kelly Torgelson, revealing that "she was concerned for her safety, that she was being stalked."

Kelly would receive Jodi's letter in the mail on June 27th, 1995 at her home in Mississippi. The day that Jodi would be abducted.

"Jodi had reported that that a man in a pickup truck stopped and eyeballed her," Powell said. "This creeped her out. She felt as if someone was after her. So that is another theory that we have to go on in the case. Because of her position in the media and being a very attractive female, she was prone to have any nut ball start to fantasize and stalk her."

NO BODY, NO EVIDENCE

The investigators continued to grasp at straws while not pursuing anything against Vansice. They simply had nothing to pin him with.

Desperate for answers, the detectives and members of Jodi's family would meet with psychics in November of 1997.

"Psychics would be called upon a lot during the 1980s and 1990s," Powell said. "It was simply a sign of desperation from everyone involved. They needed anything, just anybody with some type of answer. So these charlatans would come in and they would go through the motions. When that happens, you know that the investigators have absolutely nothing."

Jodi's disappearance would leave her co-workers at KIMT devastated. Some left the business while others moved to other stations. Not one colleague that worked with Jodi during her tenure at KIMT remains with the station.

Wolfram, Jodi's friend and fellow broadcaster, would leave KIMT a few months after Jodi disappeared.

"They called me into the office and I thought they had found Jodi," Wolfram recalled. "Otherwise, why would all these people be in the office than to share that information. But there was talk on the internet

- chat rooms - he claimed he knew who had abducted Jodi. Gruesome details. Then the reason they had brought me in was the last communication was that Robin Wolfram would be next. From that point on - I had a police escort at night. From that point forward, I look at life differently. I think I used to look at life in rose colored glasses and everyone had a pure heart like Jodi. I realized evil exists right next door to good. It's like a veil. You reach your hand across to experience it. And it's not that easy."

NEW LEADS, MORE FALSE HOPES

Jodi's case would remain in the public eye and garnered renewed interest on the 20th year anniversary of her disappearance.

In a bizarre twist, photocopies of Jodi's personal diary were anonymously mailed to a local newspaper in June of 2008. The journal was eighty-four pages long and sent to the Mason City Globe Gazette. The diary had been placed in a large envelope with no return address. Days later, however, the sender had come forward.

It was the wife of the former Mason City Police Chief.

Her motive for sending the copy to the newspaper remains unclear.

JODI'S JOURNAL

Jodi would start "journaling" after she purchased Anthony Robbins Success program.

Her entries would reveal some of her personal thoughts and how she prioritized things in terms of work, family, and friends. Throughout the pages, she expressed her love for travel, socializing and her search for someone to share her life with.

"Remember," one of her first entries read, "there is no time better than now to begin practicing being the best I can be and living the way I want to live."

Jodi would continue to write about her goals and desire to get the "Huisentruit name out." She listed Paula Zahn and Kathy Gifford as her role models.

She wrote about her dating life briefly, talking about male friends and her love for dancing. She had met a man she liked during a cruise she had taken with her mother. "Why do I get hooked so fast?" she asked in one entry. "I'm lonely here at times and would like to have someone to share my life with. Sure I meet men — but none that really strikes me, or who follows thru."

"My No. 1 goal is to get a new job," she wrote in April 1995, two months before her disappearance.

"I'm recovering from Memorial Day Weekend, unbelievable — Indy 500 — a time of my life. Partied with so many wonderful people — Mario Andretti (world class racer), Joe Dumars (Detroit Pistons basketball player) and Tim Allen (TV star from 'Home Improvement'). Had an incredible weekend."

The latter part of her entries focused more on her activities as opposed to her goals.

"I stayed in Mason City this weekend to regroup, gather my thoughts and goals, read! And have Jodi time. I've enjoyed it. Church is very important to me as is putting myself and family ... at the top. I'm starting fresh at work this week — getting up at 3 a.m. — best newscast in the world — top 10 market — I really think I'll market myself for AZ. — see what they think about my accent. Or I'll move down there to produce."

Her final three entries all mention John Vansice.

"What a weekend, Surprise," Jodi wrote on June 11, 1995. "My Mason City/Clear Lake friends thru a big party for me! At a lounge, wild. It was in Clear Lake. They had a 16 gal keg – huge cake (with a skier) so much left. John Van Sice grilled 150 pork burgers, we were dancing on tables...dancing everywhere...Everyone had a ball. Video camera was rolling, cameras were clicking – oh what fun! Life is so good. The party made me feel so good."

"Last night John,...and I went to the Glen Miller Orchestra in Belmond," Jodi wrote on June 13th, 1995. "I have so many great viewers. People are so kind. This nice weather has me wild. I bought a new Mazda Miata, simply love it."

"Got home from a weekend road trip to Iowa City," Jodi wrote in her final entry. "oh we had fun! It was wild, partying and water skiing. We skied at the Coralville Res. I'm improving on the skis — hips up, lean, etc. John's son Trent gave me some great ski tip advice. Today, Sunday, it was raining in Mason City so didn't get any skiing in. I love it, it's addicting." Later on in the entry she wrote about her desire to move on from KIMT. "Great friends but professionally, I'm fed up. It's difficult finding a new job and I'm confused about agent and what to do."

The journals didn't reveal any clues that furthered the investigation. It remains a head-scratcher as to why the wife of the former police chief would forward the journal to the newspaper.

"The journals said a lot about Jodi's character," Powell said. "Reading through it is heartbreaking because you realize how much she loved her life, her family, and friends. She was on the road to self-improvement and listened to Tony Robbins' success tapes. She aspired to beyond what she was doing. She wanted to make her mark."

NEW SUSPECT

One new suspect that did emerge in recent years was serial rapist Tony Dejuan Jackson. Jackson was twenty-one years old at the time of Huisentruit's abduction and is now serving a life sentence in Minnesota for raping three women in 1997.

He was questioned about the crime and denied ever meeting Huisentruit or seeing her in public.

His former friend, however, stated otherwise.

Speaking anonymously, this friend would tell the Minneapolis news station KMSP that he had met Jackson because their girlfriends at the time were good friends. The source described an occasion where Jackson had invited him to get drinks where he knew Jodi was a regular.

The two then arrived at the South Bridge Lounge where they saw Jodi sitting at the bar.

He stated that Jackson walked right up to Jodi and began talking to her but he didn't hear the gist of their conversation.

Jackson was living in Mason City at the time and was attending North Iowa Community College. He hosted his own student talk show and wanted to pursue a career in broadcasting.

His friend thought that Jackson simply wanted to get career advice from Jodi not really thinking anything of their conversation until years later.

"My gut tells me that he probably did it," Jackson's friend said. "After all the stuff he's done since."

This suspicion of Jackson is corroborated with a neighbor who went out jogging early in the morning. She stated that the morning before she saw a young African American man, riding a bike outside the complex. He started biking ride beside her and she was spooked by him as it was so early in the morning.

Jackson would eventually be connected to over six sexual assaults on women from North Iowa to the St. Paul area in Minnesota.

He would arm himself with handcuffs, duct tape, mask and a gun as he stalked his victims. He threatened to kill his victims when they would not submit to him. One of his victims was eventually able to identify him as she worked with Jackson at a restaurant.

Jackson would write rap songs in prison that contained the lyric "stiffin' around Tiffin." Authorities believed that he may be referring to a silo in Tiffin, Iowa which he may have dumped her body. He had also told a cellmate that he was involved with a kidnapping of a news anchor.

Mason City police would not charge him, however, and it remains unclear why the eliminated him as a suspect.

As of this writing, John Vansice remains the primary person of interest. He has since moved to Phoenix, Arizona.

Jodi would be declared legally dead in May of 2001.